Sold Out for God

Neil T. Anderson
Robert L. Saucy
and Dave Park

HARVEST HOUSE PUBLISHERS
Eugene, Oregon 97402

Acknowledgments

We would like to thank Harvest House Publishers,
especially Bob Hawkins Jr., Carolyn McCready,
LaRae Weikert, Betty Fletcher,
Barbara Gordon, and Gary Lineburg.
Thank you for sharing our vision
to help youth discover their freedom in Christ.

Contents

The Refiner's Fire

Be holy, because I am holy.
—1 PETER 1:16

Father, in the Name of Jesus, baptize me with the Holy Spirit and fire until sanctification is made real in my life.[1]
—OSWALD CHAMBERS

This book is about God's radical pursuit to make you like His Son, Jesus, and our pursuit to be holy like Jesus. It is about sinners becoming saints and children of wrath becoming children of God. The theological term for this change is *sanctification*. The command given by God to every one of His children is "be holy, because I am holy" (1 Peter 1:16). We are forgiven, but we have not yet been perfected. There is no more important work in any youth group than sanctification. Paul says, "We proclaim him, admonishing and teaching everyone with all wisdom, so that we may present everyone perfect in Christ. To this end I labor, struggling with all his energy, which so powerfully works in me" (Colossians 1:28,29).

"It is God's will that you should be sanctified" (1 Thessalonians 4:3). Everything else is secondary to God. He will certainly guide you concerning college and career choices, but His primary concern isn't whether you are a carpenter, engineer, or missionary. It's *what kind* of carpenter, engineer, or missionary you are. In fact, He may find it necessary to sacrifice your career in order to conform you to the image of God. It is character before career and maturity before ministry.

With all the sin in our churches and youth groups today, there can be no Bible truth more important to understand than sanctification. The world, the flesh, and the devil will pull out all the stops and make every effort to stop this process in your life, but we are committed to helping you understand God's desire for you to grow in Christ. Everything we have to say can be summarized by one verse: "Which is Christ in you, the hope of glory" (Colossians 1:27). We believe the Holy Spirit will lead you into all truth, and that truth will set you free to be all that God calls you to be.

The Nobel Peace Prize is the supreme award given to those who have made an exceptional contribution to the betterment of the world. Other Nobel prizes are given to those who have made outstanding contributions in the arts and sciences. There is a story about the Nobel prizes that is rarely told.

> Alfred Nobel, a Swedish chemist, made his fortune by inventing powerful explosives and licensing the formula to governments to make weapons. One day Nobel's brother died, and by accident a newspaper printed an obituary notice for Alfred instead of his deceased brother.
>
> It identified Alfred as the inventor of dynamite who made his fortune by enabling armies to achieve new levels of mass destruction. Nobel had the unique opportunity to read his own obituary in his lifetime and see how he would be remembered. He was shocked to think that this is what his life would add up to: the merchant of death and destruction.
>
> He then took his fortune and used it to establish awards for accomplishments contributing to life rather than death. And today Nobel is remembered for his contribution to peace and human achievement—not explosives.[2]

If you were able to read your own obituary, would it tell a story of selfishness or selflessness? A life lived for the glory of God or self-glorification? One day each one of us will stand before Jesus and the judgment seat of God. How will your life be reviewed?

Have you made the decision to let God be God? Do you desire more than anything to be the person He created you to be? Are you convinced that the will of God is good, acceptable, and perfect for you—even *before* you know for certain what it is? (See Romans 12:2.) Be assured that God loves His children, and He has no plans for you that aren't good, although you will surely undergo some times of testing in order that you may be purified. We have been warned in 1 Peter 4:12-14 (THE MESSAGE):

> Friends, when life gets really difficult, don't jump to the conclusion that God isn't on the job. Instead, be glad that you are in the very thick of what Christ experienced. This is a spiritual refining process, with glory just around the corner. If you're abused because of Christ, count yourself fortunate. It's the Spirit of God and his glory in you that brought you to the notice of others.

The Refiner's fire is necessary in order for the Potter to transform His earthen vessels back into His image. You will be tempted to believe it isn't worth it, but it is. Don't sacrifice eternity to satisfy the flesh. There is heaven to be gained and hell to avoid. You have been chosen by the King of kings and Lord of lords to be His child. You've been set aside from all other creation to do His will, which is good, acceptable, and perfect. The songwriter said it well:

> *Refiner's fire,*
> *My heart's one desire,*
> *Is to be holy*
> *Set apart for You, Lord....*
> *Ready to do Your will.*[3]

*The heavens declare
the glory of God;
the skies proclaim the
work of his hands.*

—PSALM 19:1

Awesome, Holy Design

When God created man in His own image He was saying "man will be unlike anything I created. No other created being has a mind to know Me. A heart to love Me. Therefore no other created being has a destiny like this created being has. We'll make Him distinct. Only humans will have imago Dei, the image of God, stamped on them." What a privileged position![1]

—*Charles Swindoll*

"Well, who do you think you are?" "It can't be done!" "That's impossible!" "What are you some kind of religious fanatic?"

Maybe you have heard some of this kind of negative talk when you've talked about wanting to live a holy life. Our world is full of it. While it's true that apart from Christ we can do nothing, with Him we can do all things—especially His will. And while we will never obtain sinless perfection, we do have the power to do whatever God asks us to do. Consider the story of Bishop Wright.

11

In the year 1870, the Methodist churches in Indiana were having their annual conference. At one point, the president of the college where they were meeting addressed the group. He told them they were living in a very exciting time of great invention and that he believed, for example, that man would someday fly through the air like the birds.

The presiding bishop didn't think much of this statement. As a matter of fact, he called it heresy and said that the Bible says that flight was reserved for the angels and not for mere mortal man. His comments killed the meeting's excitement.

When the bishop got home, he told his family about what the president of the college had said and how ridiculous it was. But his two young sons, Wilbur and Orville, looked at things a little differently than old dad. They had a different perspective than their father, Bishop Wright. And of course you already know the rest of the story—how the Wright brothers invented the first flying machine. But I wonder, Would the Wright brothers have invented the airplane if they had not had a vision planted in their heads by one not-so-visionary father?[2]

The Wright brothers used a negative voice to spur them on to new and impossible inventions. You have probably heard the same kind of negative talk from friends and maybe even family members. Those voices can leave us feeling weak and helpless, but why not use them the way the Wright brothers did? To move you to believe what Jesus says about you? We have the Word of God—the truth—to spur us on to live differently. We live in an exciting time. Jesus is coming back someday soon. Why not dare to take Jesus at His Word and live a holy life!

We are not just globs of clay that can be molded into whatever our parents or teachers want us to be.

Although we start out physically and spiritually messed up, Jesus wants to show us how we can live to honor Him. Physically, we are born relatively helpless compared to the creatures in the animal kingdom. You can't help but marvel when you observe a little lamb, who was coiled for weeks in the womb of its mother, wobble to its feet only minutes after being born. How do those little guys do that? Physically, we humans develop at a much slower pace. Yet our brain size is a lot larger, which allows us to take part in our own growth in many ways that animals cannot.

Paul refers to growth in the spiritual dimension as the "inner man," and this growth is totally different than physical growth (check out 2 Corinthians 4:16). In contrast to animals, whose entire development is controlled by divine instinct, we are created by God to play a much more significant role in our spiritual growth. Although our growing up and maturing is influenced by our parents, friends, and teachers, the most significant role is played by ourselves. Many people will help or hinder us in the pursuit of God and holiness, but nobody can stop us from being the people God has called us to be. This ability to participate in the shaping of our own lives is rooted in the biblical truth that we are created in "the image of God" (Genesis 1:27).

We are not just globs of clay that can be molded into whatever our parents or teachers want us to be. Rather, those who raise or teach us would be wise to discover the gifts, talents, and unique personality that God has already created in each of us. No amount of nurturing can turn a tulip into a rose, but a lot of love and tender care can greatly influence the brilliance of a tulip's blossoms. When it comes to spiritual growth, it is as though we possess a spiritual DNA molecule that God has known from the foundation of the world. "We are God's workmanship, created in Christ Jesus to do good works, which God prepared in advance for us to do" (Ephesians 2:10).

You will never read a birth announcement that says Mr. and Mrs. John Doe gave birth to a doctor, a pro football player, an engineer, or a lawyer. Each one will achieve his or her professional status because of God-given abilities, personal choices, and hard work. In a limited sense, God has called each of us to participate in the development of what He intends us to become. This is a great privilege and an awesome responsibility, for no other human being can determine our ultimate destiny. Created with the capacity to think (Yes, contrary to the way you may have been treated, you can think!), we are the main human factor involved in the process of shaping ourselves and determining our destiny:

> Whoever sows a thought, reaps an action;
> Whoever sows an action, reaps a habit;
> Whoever sows a habit, reaps a lifestyle;
> Whoever sows a lifestyle, reaps a destiny.

The Biblical Challenge to Grow

The world may say, "You can't grow; you can't be like Jesus," but the world says a lot of dumb things. For example, in a briefing room at an American air base during World War II there were posters with the following inscription:

> By all known laws which can be proved on paper and in the wind tunnel, the bumblebee cannot fly. The size of his wings in relation to his body, according to aeronautical and mathematical science, simply means he cannot fly. It is an impossibility. But of course, the bumblebee doesn't know about the rules so he goes ahead and flies anyway.[3]

We need to hear what *Jesus* says we can and cannot do and not what the world or the flesh—and certainly not the devil—says we can or cannot do.

Check out the parables of the talents (Matthew 25:14-30) and the pounds (Luke 19:12-26 KJV). Jesus teaches that we have all been given certain gifts and abilities for life, and we will be held accountable for what we have done with what God has entrusted to us. Even if you don't feel like you've been given very much to work with in terms of talents and abilities, the Bible makes it clear that you have everything you need to live a godly life. Ask yourself a personal question: Are you cheating to get ahead? Or are you using what God has given you to become what He has created you to be? This old story demonstrates the point we're trying to make.

> Once there was an emperor in the Far East who was growing old and knew it was coming time to choose his successor. Instead of choosing one of his assistants or one of his own children, he decided to do something

different. He called all the young people in the kingdom together one day. He said, "It has come time for me to step down and to choose the next emperor. I have decided to choose one of you." The kids were shocked! But the emperor continued. "I am going to give each one of you a seed today. One seed. It is a very special seed. I want you to go home, plant the seed, water it, and come back here one year from today with what you have grown from this one seed. I will then judge the plants that you bring to me, and the one I choose will be the next emperor of the kingdom!"

There was one boy named Ling who was there that day and he, like the others, received a seed. He went home and excitedly told his mother the whole story. She helped him get a pot and some planting soil, and he planted the seed and watered it carefully. Every day he would water it and watch to see if it had grown. After about three weeks, some of the other youths began to talk about their seeds and the plants that were beginning to grow.

Ling kept going home and checking his seed, but nothing ever grew. Three weeks, four weeks, five weeks went by. Still nothing. By now all the others were talking about their plants, but Ling didn't have a plant, and he felt like a failure. Six months went by—still nothing in Ling's pot. He just knew he had killed his seed. Everyone else had trees and tall plants, but he had nothing. Ling didn't say anything to his friends, however. He just kept waiting for his seed to grow.

A year finally went by and all the youths of the kingdom brought their plants to the emperor for inspection. Ling told his mother that he wasn't going to take an empty pot. But she encouraged him to go, and to take his pot and be honest about what happened. Ling felt sick to his stomach, but he knew his mother was right. He took his empty pot to the palace.

When Ling arrived, he was amazed at the variety of plants grown by all the other youths. They were beautiful—in all shapes and sizes. Ling put his empty pot on the floor, and many of the other kids laughed at him. A few felt sorry for him and just said, "Hey, nice try."

When the emperor arrived, he surveyed the room and greeted the young people. Ling just tried to hide in the back. "My, what great plants, trees, and flowers you have grown," said the emperor. "Today one of you will be appointed the next emperor!"

All of a sudden the emperor spotted Ling at the back of the room with his empty pot. He ordered his guards to bring him to the front. Ling was terrified. "The emperor knows I'm a failure! Maybe he will have me killed!"

When Ling got to the front, the emperor asked his name.

"My name is Ling," he replied.

All the kids were laughing and making fun of him. The emperor asked everyone to quiet down. He looked at Ling and then announced to the crowd, "Behold your new emperor! His name is Ling!"

Ling couldn't believe it. He couldn't even grow his seed. How could he be the new emperor?

Then the emperor said, "One year ago today, I gave everyone here a seed. I told you to take the seed, plant it, water it, and bring it back to me today. But I gave you all boiled seeds which would not grow. All of you, except Ling, have brought me trees and plants and flowers. When you found that the seed would not grow, you substituted another seed for the one I gave you. Ling was the only one with the courage and honesty to bring me a pot with my seed in it. Therefore, he is the one who will be the new emperor!"[4]

The Bible reveals that apart from Christ we can do nothing (John 15:5). The grace of God and human responsibility are two important parts of human growth and potential. In addition, God has provided all the resources we need in order to become all that He created us to be (2 Peter 1:3). We cannot become someone we are not... nor should we try.

The entrance of sin into God's created world brought a destructive power that kills and destroys. Sin's presence was introduced by a magnificent angel whose pride and rebellion led to his downfall: "How you have fallen from heaven, O morning star, son of the dawn! You have been cast down to the earth, you who once laid low the nations!" (Isaiah 14:12). Satan took many other angelic beings down with him in this rebellion. Then he succeeded in deceiving Eve, which resulted in the fall of mankind: "Therefore, just as sin entered the world through one man, and death through sin, and in this way death came to all men, because all sinned" (Romans 5:12).

Enough with the bad news, there's some good news! The prince of darkness, death, and destruction has been defeated by the Author of life and light. John writes, "The thief [Satan] comes only to steal and kill and destroy; I have come that [you] may have life, and have it to the full" (John 10:10). God, through Christ, unleashed a greater power than sin that allows us to grow toward the fullness of life for which we were created. Paul writes, "For if, by the trespass of the one man, death reigned through that one man, how much more will those who receive God's abundant provision of grace and of the gift of righteousness reign in life through the one man, Jesus Christ. . . . Just as sin reigned in death, so also grace might reign through righteousness to bring eternal life through Jesus Christ our Lord" (Romans 5:17, 21).

Have you ever noticed how tiny babies already know how to nurse? Have you ever seen the cravings that growing babies have for bottles of milk? They let you know if they're hungry, don't they? The natural craving that the body has for self-preservation and growth, coupled with the realization that the food is good, causes infants to want more and more and to cry in protest if they don't get it. Even the basic instincts of a child reveal that all created beings are designed to grow.

> A group of tourists were traveling through Europe visiting historical sites. They were impressed that so many small villages were the birthplace of great artists, poets, composers, and political leaders. While the group was strolling through a particularly picturesque village, one of the tourists approached a man who was sitting in front of a building and asked, "Excuse me, but ...were any great men or women born in this village?"
>
> The old man thought for a moment and replied, "No. Only great babies!"[5]

Peter writes, "Like newborn babies, crave pure spiritual milk, so that by it you may grow up in your salvation, now that you have tasted that the Lord is good" (1 Peter 2:2). The Bible challenges us to grow. We are to grow in our faith (2 Corinthians 10:15), in the grace and knowledge of our Savior (2 Peter 3:18), and in love (Ephesians 4:16). In the Bible, growth is frequently expressed as a process of building. We are told to build ourselves up in our faith (Jude 20) and build up one another (1 Thessalonians 5:11). Our growth is not just an individual matter. It takes place with other believers as the church is being "built together into a dwelling of God in the Spirit" (Ephesians 2:22 NASB). The church—or the body—"builds itself up in love" as each part does its share (Ephesians 4:16, see also verse 12). The growth of the church collectively takes place only as individuals in the church grow. Of course, all of this building is enabled only by the grace of God (Acts 20:32).

We are being "perfected"; therefore, "let us purify ourselves from everything that contaminates body and spirit, perfecting holiness out of reverence for God" (Galatians 3:3 NASB; 2 Corinthians 7:1). We are also being renewed or made new (2 Corinthians 4:16; Ephesians 4:23; Colossians 3:10; Titus 3:5). This renewal includes the transformation of our minds and eventually affects our entire being (see Romans 12:2-8). "We all, with unveiled face beholding as in a mirror the glory of the Lord, are being transformed into the same image from glory to glory, just as from the Lord, the Spirit" (2 Corinthians 3:18 NASB). Our growth is in every dimension of salvation, but especially in our faith and knowledge of Christ. Believers are growing toward a destiny characterized by the fullness of Christ's life and character (see Colossians 1:28).

Being like Christ means being like God. We are being renewed in the image of our Creator (Ephesians 4:24). It is God's plan to restore a fallen human race back to its original design. He will faithfully do His part, but what if we don't shoulder our responsibility? Will we grow beyond our salvation experience? If we don't grow up, what effect will that have on the church and our youth groups? You may feel like you don't want to grow up right now: "Hey, I'm still young and have my whole life ahead of me, and a little time in the world won't make that much difference"; "I'll get my act together and take my Christianity seriously when I go to college or get married." Take a lesson from the Jewish culture: They declare a young boy to be a man at about 13 years of age. Why? Because he's old enough to internalize what God's Word says about him and live according to its precepts. And so are you.

Viewing God's Holiness

Every child of God begins his or her spiritual journey as a babe in Christ. It is one thing to "be" in Christ, and yet another to become all that He has created us to be. It's kind of like the army commercial: "Be all that you can be." Anyone can watch the commercial while sitting on the couch at home eating a bag of potato chips and drinking Dr Pepper, but only the ones that actually join the army are going to receive the training that can produce a top-notch soldier.

Personalities, gifts, and talents will determine our own uniqueness in the body of Christ and determine what we should and can do for His glory—but there is one pursuit that we all hold in common: We are to be holy as He is holy (see 1 Peter 1:16). Because we are in the process of conforming to the image of God, we need to know what we are trying to become like.

The most significant characteristic of God is His holiness. In the Old Testament, the people of Israel proclaimed, "He is holy" (Psalm 99:3). The psalmist declared, "Holy and awesome is his name" (Psalm 111:9). The name of God is His person and reflects all that He is and does. Isaiah especially refers to God as "the Holy One of Israel" (see Isaiah 1:4; 5:19,24) or, simply, "the Holy One" (Isaiah 40:25; 41:14,16).

Of all of the words used to describe God, *holy* speaks most directly to His deity. Hosea 11:9 says, "I am God, and not man—the Holy One among you." There is none or nothing equal to "the Holy One" (Exodus 15:11). Because God cannot swear an oath by anything higher, He swears by His own self (Amos 6:8; see also Hebrews 6:13), which is the equivalent of swearing by "his holiness" (Amos 4:2; Psalm 89:35).

To speak of God's holiness is first of all to speak of His distinctness or His separateness from all other things. He is holy in His power over all creation. "He is exalted over all the nations," the psalmist declares, and therefore "he is holy" (Psalm 99:2,3; see also verses 5,9). He is "the high and lofty One...whose name is holy" and who lives in "a high and holy place" (Isaiah 57:15).

As the Holy One who lives above and beyond all creation, God is also separate from the evil that defiles the creation. He is separate as the Creator, and He is separate from sin. His holiness includes absolute moral perfection. Isaiah says, "The holy God will show himself holy by his righteousness" (Isaiah 5:16). As the Holy One, His "eyes are too pure to look on evil...[or] tolerate wrong" (Habakkuk 1:13). To sin is to spurn the Holy One (Isaiah 1:4). Only the person who has "clean hands and a pure heart" can stand in the Lord's holy place (Psalm 24:3,4; see also Leviticus 16:30).

When you hear what God's Word says about God's holiness, you might be thinking, "I'm supposed to be or become holy like God? How?" Obviously we can't become holy apart from the grace of God. There is no way humanly possible that we can become like God—much less stand in His presence. We were born dead in our trespasses and sins and "were by nature children of wrath" (see Ephesians 2:1,3 NASB). What hope do we have? God is too pure, too perfect, too awesome! The psalmist declares, "Holy and awesome is his name" (Psalm 111:9). There is none like "the Holy One" (see Isaiah 40:25). "There is no one holy like the LORD" (1 Samuel 2:2).

The fearful nature of God's holiness is seen in Isaiah's vision of the heavenly beings around God's throne calling to one another, "Holy, holy, holy is the LORD Almighty; the whole earth is full of his glory" (Isaiah 6:3; also check out Revelation 4:8).

No human has fully seen God, but Scripture does reveal that some individuals were allowed to experience an unusual sense of His presence. Moses prayed, "'Show me your glory.' And the LORD said, 'I will cause all my goodness to pass in front of you. . . . But,' he said, 'you cannot see my face, for no one may see me and live'" (Exodus 33:18-20). Moses fell on his face and worshiped God, and his physical countenance radiated the glory of God.

When I (Dave) was about six years old I remember watching *The Wizard of Oz* on television. I was terrified of the green witch, the wicked witch of the west. I watched every scene that she appeared in through the hole in the afghan blanket we had on our couch. The fear or reverence of God is to be even greater. Nothing—and I mean *nothing*—can so immediately and profoundly affect the character and behavior of mankind more than to be confronted with the glory of God, which is a manifestation of His presence. People all over the world have cowered in fear at the presence of demonic manifestations, but their fear would pale in comparison to what they would experience in God's presence.

When Isaiah saw the glory of God's holy nature in his vision, the temple shook and the prophet became fearful. But it was more than the awesome splendor of God's holy nature that affected the prophet. It was the absolute purity of God's holiness and His character that overwhelmed Isaiah and brought crushing conviction of his own sin— "Woe is me, for I am ruined!" (Isaiah 6:5 NASB). Centuries later, when Peter witnessed the awesomeness of God on display in Jesus, "he fell at Jesus' knees and said, 'Go away from me, Lord; I am a sinful man!'" (Luke 5:8). Likewise, if we were brought into the Lord's presence, we would all crumble at His feet with overwhelming conviction. Christians who are actively aware of God's constant presence in their lives are acutely aware of their own sin. Those who don't practice such awareness often see the sins of others and not their own.

The holiness of God and His acts rightly bring terror on His enemies (see Exodus 15:6-15; Revelation 15:4). The writer of Hebrews warned those who turn away from God that "it is a dreadful thing to fall into the hands of the living God" (10:31). Yet it is out of the very nature of this Holy One that salvation comes to us (see Isaiah 54:5). What God said to His covenant people in the Old Testament, He says to all those who receive Him in His holy nature: "All my compassion is aroused. I will not carry out my fierce anger. . . . For I am God, and not man—the Holy One among you. I will not come in wrath" (Hosea 11:8,9). God's great acts as a redeemer lead to awe-inspired praise from His people. Their response is to "acknowledge the holiness of the Holy One of Jacob, and . . . stand in awe of the God of Israel" (Isaiah 29:23). The psalmist similarly declared, "Worship the LORD in the splendor of his holiness; tremble before him, all the earth" (Psalm 96:9).

Set Apart for God

Because God is holy, everything associated with Him is also holy or sanctified (set apart). The first use of *holy* in the Bible occurs when Moses meets God at the burning bush. Moses is warned, "Do not come any closer. . . . Take off your sandals, for the place where you are standing is holy ground" (Exodus 3:5). The second use of *holy* appears in Exodus 12:16 (NASB) in reference to the "holy assembly" of God's people, who were called to celebrate the Passover.

This second use points to the Bible's most frequent use of *holy* in connection with God's people. Entering into a covenant with them at Mount Sinai, God declared, "You will be for me . . . a holy nation" (Exodus 19:6). Frequently God reminds His people that they are to be holy because they belong to Him (who is holy): "Be holy because I, the LORD your God, am holy" (Leviticus 19:2; see also 11:44; 20:26; 1 Peter 1:16). They were God's holy people because, as God reminds them, "I have set you apart [sanctified you] from the nations to be my own" (Leviticus 20:26).

In the Old Testament, the priests who ministered in the worship of God on behalf of the people were holy. While all were God's holy people, these priests came near to God in a special way and were set apart more than the others. Even the priests' food was holy (Leviticus 22:10).

The tabernacle (the temporary tent used for sacrifices) and temple (where God dwelled among His people), along with their furnishings, were considered holy (Exodus 29:43,44; Matthew 23:17,19). The activities associated with worshiping God, including the offerings, were also holy (Exodus 29:26,27). The firstborn males of both people and animals were all consecrated to God, or made holy (Exodus 13:2; Deuteronomy 15:19). Particular days or years were set apart to God and made holy, such as the Sabbath (Genesis 2:3), fast days (Joel 1:14), and the year of jubilee (Leviticus 25:10). Holiness was attributed to heaven, God's dwelling place (Psalm 20:6), God's throne (Psalm 47:8), Zion, God's "holy hill" (Psalm 2:6), and to Scripture (Romans 1:2). Even the kiss of greeting among Christians was called "a holy kiss" (Romans 16:16).

It was important for God's people to know the difference between what was holy and what was sinful, and what was clean and unclean. Instructions were given to the priests to "distinguish between the holy and the common, between the unclean and the clean" (Leviticus 10:10) and teach it to the people (Ezekiel 44:23). To fail to maintain this distinction and treat something that was holy as though it were common was to profane or desecrate the holy thing (Exodus 31:14). For God's people to live in sin was to profane God's name before others (Proverbs 30:8,9; Ezekiel 36:20-23).

Called to Be Holy

If all that is associated with God is holy, then the logical and necessary conclusion is that holiness must characterize His people, young and old. A personal and intimate relationship with God is the essence of life. This is what Jesus meant when He said, "This is eternal life: that they may know you, the only true God, and Jesus Christ, whom you have sent" (John 17:3). To "know you," as used in this statement, means the knowledge of personal experience. To know a person in this sense is not to have mere knowledge *about* that person; rather, it is to know that person as a friend—to be in an intimate relationship so that your lives influence each other.

To have eternal life is to have an intimate friendship with the holy God, the source of all true life. Because God desires to give His life to His people in abundance, He calls them to holiness and purity and provides instructions for living a holy life. When the Lord told His people in the Old Testament to maintain a distinction between common and holy things, He declared, "I am the LORD, who brought you up from the land of Egypt, to be your God: thus you shall be holy for I am holy" (Leviticus 11:44 NASB).

When God's people pursued holiness, they exalted God's holiness. Just as disobedience stains God's name, obedience sanctifies or declares God's name holy. God said, "You shall keep My commandments, and do them: I am the LORD. And you shall not profane My holy name, but I will be sanctified among the sons of Israel: I am the LORD who sanctifies you" (Leviticus 22:31,32 NASB). First Peter 3:15 tells us to "sanctify Christ as Lord in [our] hearts."

Many of the specific laws about clean and unclean things, such as foods, came to an end with Christ's work on the cross, but the principle of holiness that these laws symbolized remains strong for the New Testament believer. The apostle Peter wrote, "As obedient children, do not conform to the evil desires you had when you lived in ignorance. But just as he who called you is holy, so be holy in all you do; for it is written: 'Be holy, because I am holy'" (1 Peter 1:14-16). The apostle Paul called for us to live a pure life: "This is the will of God, your sanctification" (1 Thessalonians 4:3 NASB). And, "Therefore, having these promises, beloved, let us cleanse ourselves from all defilement of flesh and spirit, perfecting holiness in the fear of God" (2 Corinthians 7:1 NASB; see also 1 Thessalonians 5:23).

Holiness or sanctification is not simply commanded for the believer. It is, as we've said before, clearly linked to the daily experience of God in our lives. Sometimes we like to call our own shots in life, but we should pay heed to this old sea story:

> A battleship was taking part in maneuvers during severe weather for several days. One evening as night fell on the foggy sea, the captain decided to stay on the bridge to keep an eye on

things. The lookout on the wing of the bridge reported a light bearing on the starboard bow.

The captain asked if it were steady or moving astern. The lookout replied, "Steady, Captain." That means they were on a collision course.

That captain called to the signalman, "Signal that ship to change its course 20 degrees to the north."

Back came this signal: "Change your course 20 degrees to the south."

The captain said, "Send: I am a captain. Change your course 20 degrees to the north."

The reply came back, "I am a seaman second class. Change your course 20 degrees south immediately."

By this time the captain was furious. He said, "Send: I am a battleship. Change your course 20 degrees north."

Back came the message, "Change your course 20 degrees south. I am a lighthouse."[6]

We are called to holiness. The psalmist asks, "Who may ascend the hill of the Lord? Who may stand in his holy place? He who has clean hands and a pure heart. . . . He will receive blessing from the Lord and vindication from God his Savior" (Psalm 24:3-5).

God is not only the King who allows the holy one into His presence, He is also the host of His home who invites the believer to dwell with Him: "Lord, who may dwell in your sanctuary? Who may live on your holy hill?" (Psalm 15:1). Eugene Peterson captures the thought of this verse: "God, who gets invited to dinner at your place? How do we get on your guest list?" (The Message). The very next verse answers the question by citing the qualities of holiness: "He who walks with integrity, and works righteousness, and speaks truth in his heart" (Psalm 15:2 NASB).

The importance of holiness in the believer's life is evident also in the way that holiness is linked to life itself. The apostle Paul declared, "If you are living according to the flesh [according to your own sinful will, which is contrary to God's holiness], you must die; but if by the Spirit you are putting to death the deeds of the body, you will live" (Romans 8:13 NASB). So sanctification, or growth in holiness, is viewed as an essential element in the Christian's life. After stating that the outcome of the things that we did before we came to Christ is death, Paul goes on to say, "But now that you have been set free from sin and have become slaves to God, the benefit you reap leads to holiness, and the result is eternal life" (Romans 6:22). Between the initial salvation of being set free from sin and the final state of eternal life there is the process of growth in holiness or sanctification. The Christian is chosen by God "to be saved through [the process of] the sanctifying work of the Spirit and through belief in the truth" (2 Thessalonians 2:13).

Clearly the Bible reveals that God has called us to be holy as He is holy. Without this holiness, we will die and end up in hell. But, humanly speaking, what fun is there in being a saint? What pleasure is there in living a holy life? Why should we bow to some higher authority when we can be our own god and determine our own destiny?

> The queen of England often visits Bob Morrow Castle. On one occasion when she was walking by herself, it started to rain. She rushed to the shelter of the nearest cottage. The lady who came to the door was really ticked off that someone would bother her at that time of the morning. She opened the door a few inches and barked, "What do you want?"

The queen didn't introduce herself. She merely asked, "May I borrow an umbrella?"

"Just a minute," grumbled the woman. She slammed the door, was gone for a moment, and returned with the rattiest umbrella she could find, one with broken ribs and holes. She pushed it through the door and said, "Here."

The queen of England thanked her and went on her way with the ragged umbrella.

The next morning, the queen's full escort, dressed in full uniform, pulled up in front of the cottage. One of the escorts knocked on the door and returned the umbrella to the woman and said, "Madam, the queen of England thanks you." As he walked away he heard her mutter, "If I'd only known, I would have given her my best."[7]

Our King is watching, and He offers to personally guide our lives if we let Him. He reminds us that "there is a way that seems right to a man, but in the end it leads to death" (Proverbs 14:12). We deny God's holiness and refuse His wisdom when we rely on our own strength and intellect. For example, seatbelts are somewhat restrictive, yet they are designed to protect you. You may say, "I'm old enough to take care of myself. I don't need to worry about obeying any seatbelt laws because I'm a good driver." No matter who you are or what you have, your chances of surviving a major car crash improve dramatically if you use that protection.

It's easy to view the commandments of God as being restrictive, but in actuality, they are *protective*. They protect us from the god of this world (Satan) and from self-centered living, which can only lead to destruction and death. Only in the will of God can the deep longings of our hearts be fulfilled. And, contrary to what some people may think, *a holy life is* not *a boring life.* It is an exciting adventure in which we follow God into tomorrow and into an eternity that is known only by Him. What would it take for you to be happy? A new car? A gold-plated snowboard? Fame and fortune? A clear complexion? There is nothing inherently wrong with any of these things, but they will not give you what a Spirit-filled life of holiness can. Only this kind of life can give you the lasting fulfillment you long for.

Apart from God, we really don't know what is best. So how do we grow in holiness—what part do we play, and what part does God play? What helps us grow and what hinders our growth? Exploring these questions and more will help us understand how God pursues us to make us holy.

Sold Out

Matthew 25:14-20 and Luke 19:12-27

Reflect

Jesus told these two stories to help us better understand our spiritual responsibility to grow.

What are you personally responsible for in regard to spiritual growth?

What can we do on our own to help us grow spiritually? (For a clue check out John 15:5.)

What does God provide for our spiritual growth? (Check out 2 Peter 1:3.)

God's plan to restore sinful humans is at work, and He is doing His part. What happens if we don't shoulder our responsibilities?

What is the ultimate outcome of our spiritual growth? (See Ephesians 4:13.)

What challenges to grow do you find in the following verses?
2 Corinthians 10:15; Ephesians 2:19-22; Ephesians 4:16

Respond

Dear Heavenly Father, I can't even begin to imagine how holy and pure You are. You are distinct and separate from all other things; there is no one like You. You have never sinned or even had a sinful thought. You have never done anything evil or wicked. Yet You desire to seek and save the lost. Through Your Son's death and resurrection You turn sinners into saints. God, Your love is so great and overwhelming that I confess it's hard to believe, yet I know it's true. Help me seek Your presence and Your glory that I might see my sin and turn from it. In Jesus' name, amen.

Now that you have been set free from sin and have become slaves to God, the benefit you reap leads to holiness, and the result is eternal life. For the wages of sin is death, but the gift of God is eternal life in Christ Jesus our Lord.

—ROMANS 6:22,23

Spray paint won't fix rust. Band-Aids won't remove a tumor. Wax on the hood won't cure the cough of a motor. If the problem is inside, you have to go inside.[1]

—*Max Lucado*

Totally Saved and Set Apart

Slavery in the United States was abolished by the Thirteenth Amendment, December 18, 1865. How many slaves were there on December 19? In reality, none, but how many still lived like slaves? A lot! Why? Because they never learned the truth. Others knew and even believed they were free, but they chose to continue living as they had always been taught.

Many plantation owners were devastated by this proclamation of freedom. "We're ruined! Slavery has been abolished. We've lost the battle to keep our slaves," they cried.

But Satan slyly responded, "Not necessarily. As long as these people think they're still slaves, the proclamation of emancipation will have no practical effect. You don't have a legal right over them anymore, but many of them don't know it. Keep your slaves from learning the truth, and your control over them will not even be challenged."

"But what if the news spreads?"

"Don't panic. We have another barrel on our gun. We may not be able to keep them from hearing the news, but we can still keep them from understanding it. They don't call me the father of lies for nothing. We still have the potential to deceive the whole world. Just tell them they misunderstood the Thirteenth Amendment. Tell them they are *going* to be free, not that they are free already. Someday they may receive the benefits, but not now."

"But they'll expect me to say that. They won't believe me."

"Then pick out a few persuasive ones who are convinced they're still slaves, and let them do the talking for you. Remember, most of these newly freed people were born as slaves and have lived like slaves all their lives. All we have to do is to deceive them so that they still *think* like slaves. As long as they continue to do what slaves do, it will not be hard to convince them they must still be slaves. They will maintain their slave identity because of the things they do. The moment they try to profess that they are no longer slaves, just whisper in their ears, 'How can you even think you are no longer a slave when you are still doing things slaves do?' After all, we have the capacity to accuse the brethren day and night."

Years later, many slaves have still not heard the wonderful news that they have been freed, so naturally they continue to live the way they have always lived. Some slaves have heard the good news, but they evaluate it by what they are presently doing and feeling. They reason, "I'm still living in bondage, doing the same things I have always done. My experience tells me that I must not be free. I'm feeling the same way I was before the proclamation, so it must not be true. After all, feelings always tell the truth." So they continue to live according to how they feel, not wanting to be hypocrites.

We have been set free in Christ. We are no longer sinners in the hands of an angry God. We are saints in the hands of a loving God.

One former slave, however, hears the good news and receives it with great joy. He checks out the validity of the proclamation and finds out that the highest of all authorities originated the decree. Not only that, but it personally cost that authority a tremendous price, which he willingly paid so that the slave could be free. As a result, the slave's life is transformed. He correctly reasons that it would be wrong to believe his feelings and not the truth. Determined to live by what he knows to be true, his experiences begin to change rather dramatically. He realizes that his old master has no authority over him and does not need to be obeyed. He gladly serves the one who set him free.[2]

Every person that comes into this world is born dead in his or her trespasses and sins (see Ephesians 2:1). But the gospel is the "proclamation of emancipation" for every sinner. We who are Christians are no longer slaves to sin. We are now alive in Christ and dead to sin (Romans 6:11). We have been set free in Christ. We are no longer sinners in the hands of an angry God; we are saints in the hands of a loving God. We are forgiven, justified, redeemed, and born-again children of God. We may not feel like it, we may not act like it, and others may tell us that we are not—but we have been and are being sanctified in Christ.

When we were slaves to sin, we could not free ourselves. And not understanding what Christ has already accomplished for us has resulted in many Christians desperately trying to become free. On the other hand, some people are claiming a perfection that has not yet been realized. If we want to mature in our relationship with God, then we must understand the difference between what Christ has already accomplished for us and what still needs to be done. We also need to know what part Christ plays in our sanctification, and what part we play.

Freedom and Deliverance

The idea of salvation in the New Testament also carries the meaning of deliverance and freedom. Paul said, "It is for freedom that Christ has set us free. Stand firm, then, and do not let yourselves be burdened again by a yoke of slavery" (Galatians 5:1). In other words, don't put yourself back under the law as a means of relating to God because you have already been set free in Christ.

The Greek root word for salvation communicates the notion of wholeness, soundness, and health. The New Testament word for salvation helps us understand that holiness is not just getting rid of sin. Rather, holiness is *freeing* us from all the hindrances that would prevent us from being all that we were created to be. Salvation, in its broadest sense, includes deliverance from all that keeps fallen humanity from becoming complete in Christ according to God's creative design.

A lot of young people miss this important understanding of salvation. What Adam and Eve lost as a result of their sin was life. They died spiritually—that is, they lost their close communion with God and became slaves to sin. Every person since that time has been born physically alive but spiritually dead. (Physical death would also be a consequence of Adam and Eve's sin, but not for hundreds of years.)

Ever since Adam and Eve's transgression, man has searched for the purpose and meaning of life. We ask, "Who are we? Why are we here?" But because of our sin and rebellious hearts, we seek the answers from every source except God. In our quest we have "exchanged the truth of God for a lie, and worshiped and served created things rather than the Creator" (Romans 1:25). In turning away from truth, we attempt to establish our identities based on physical appearances, social status, performance, and the roles we play. We try to believe that—

Appearance + admiration = belonging
Performance + accomplishment = significance
Status + recognition = safety and security

But trying to make sense of life without God is futile. Take Solomon, for example. He appeared to have it all— power, status, and wealth. He owned the plantation! He had everything that people fight and kill for, but something was missing. And Solomon not only had the position and the opportunity to pursue the meaning of life, but he also had more God-given wisdom than any other human being. But after looking for fulfillment away from

God, he wrote his conclusions in the book of Ecclesiastes: "Meaningless! Meaningless!...Utterly meaningless! Everything is meaningless" (1:2). But it isn't supposed to be that way!

The Gift of Life

For the most part, we hear only part of the gospel message: Jesus is presented as the Messiah who died for our sins, and if we will receive Him into our hearts, He will forgive us our sins and we will get to go to heaven when we die.

Two things are wrong with that presentation. First, it gives the impression that eternal life is something we get when we die. That is not true. *Every born-again child of God has eternal life right now:* "He who has the Son has life; he who does not have the Son of God does not have life" (1 John 5:12).

Second, if you were going to save a dead person, what would you do? Give him life? If that were all you did, he would only die again. There are two requirements for saving a dead person: First, you have to cure the disease that caused him to die. The Bible says that the "wages of sin is death..." (Romans 6:23). That's why Jesus went to the cross and died for our sins. Second, the other half of the picture is completed when you finish the verse: "The gift of God is eternal life in Christ Jesus our Lord" (Romans 6:23).

Have you ever heard the story "Ragman" by Walter J. Wangerin? I (Dave) first heard it at a conference where I was speaking. Jason Nightingale performed the dramatic story from memory. (He does most things from memory. And having memorized the entire New Testament, he's ready at a moment's notice to quote whole epistles!)

Jason's a large man and, with his full beard and leather jacket, looks like someone who just jumped off a Harley Davidson motorcycle. To me Jason epitomizes this story, and he will always be the best at telling it. With his deep— and I mean *deep*—booming voice he told the story of the Ragman:

> I saw a strange sight. I stumbled upon a story most strange, like nothing my life, my street sense, my sly tongue had ever prepared me for.
>
> Hush, child. Hush, now and I will tell it to you.
>
> Even before dawn one Friday morning I noticed a young man, handsome and strong, walking the alleys of our city. He was pulling an old cart filled with clothes both bright and new, and he was calling in a clear, tenor voice: "Rags!" Ah the air was foul and the first light filthy to be crossed by such sweet music.
>
> "Rags! New rags for old! I take your tired rags! Rags!"
>
> "Now this is a wonder," I thought to myself, for the man stood six-foot-four, and his arms were like tree limbs, hard and muscular. His eyes flashed intelligence. Could he find no better job than this, to be a ragman in the inner city?
>
> I followed him. My curiosity drove me. And I wasn't disappointed.
>
> Soon the Ragman saw a woman sitting on her back porch. She was sobbing into a handkerchief, sighing and shedding a thousand tears. Her knees and elbows made a sad X. Her shoulders shook. Her heart was breaking.
>
> The Ragman stopped his cart. Quietly, he walked to the woman, stepping 'round tin cans, dead toys, and old Pampers.
>
> "Give me your rag," he said so gently, "and I'll give you another."

He slipped the handkerchief from her eyes. She looked up, and he laid across her palm a linen cloth so clean and new that it shined. She blinked from the gift to the giver.

Then, as he began to pull his cart again, the Ragman did a strange thing: He put her stained handkerchief to his own face; and then he began to weep, to sob so grievously as she had done, his shoulders shaking. Yet she was left without a tear.

"This is a wonder," I breathed to myself, and I followed the sobbing Ragman like a child who cannot turn away from mystery.

"Rags! Rags! New rags for old!"

In a little while, when the sky showed gray behind the rooftops and I could see the shredded curtains hanging out black windows, the Ragman came upon a girl whose head was wrapped in a bandage and whose eyes were empty. Blood soaked her bandage. A single line of blood ran down her cheek.

Now the tall Ragman looked upon this child with pity, and he drew a lovely yellow bonnet from his cart.

"Give me your rag," he said, tracing his own line on her cheek, "and I'll give you mine."

The child could only gaze at him while he loosened the bandage, removed it, and tied it to his own head. The bonnet he set on hers. And I gasped at what I saw: for with the bandage went the wound! Against his brow ran a darker, more substantial blood—his own!

"Rags! Rags! I take old rags!" cried the sobbing, bleeding, strong, intelligent Ragman.

The sun hurt both the sky, now, and my eyes; the Ragman seemed more and more to hurry.

"Are you going to work?" he asked a man who leaned against a telephone pole. The man shook his head.

The Ragman pressed him, "Do you have a job?"

"Are you crazy?" sneered the other. He pulled away from the pole, revealing the right sleeve of his jacket—flat, the cuff stuffed into the pocket. He had no arm.

"So," said the Ragman, "give me your jacket, and I'll give you mine."

Such quiet authority in his voice!

The one-armed man took off his jacket. So did the Ragman—and I trembled at what I saw: for the Ragman's arm stayed in its sleeve, and when the other put it on he had two good arms, thick as tree limbs; but the Ragman had only one.

"Go to work," he said.

After that he found a drunk, lying unconscious beneath an army blanket, an old man, hunched, wizened, and sick. He took that blanket and wrapped it around himself, but for the drunk he left new clothes.

And now I had to run to keep up with the Ragman. Though he was weeping uncontrollably, and bleeding freely at the forehead, pulling his cart with one arm, stumbling, falling again and again, exhausted, old, and sick, yet he went with terrible speed. On spider's legs he skittered through the alleys of the city, this mile and the next, until he came to its limits, and then he rushed beyond.

I wept to see the change in this man. I hurt to see his sorrow. And yet I needed to see where he was going in such haste, perhaps to know what drove him so.

The little old Ragman, he came to a landfill. He came to the garbage pits. And then I wanted to help him in what he did, but I hung back, hiding. He climbed a hill. With tormented labor he cleared a little space on that hill. Then he sighed. He lay down. He pillowed his head on a handkerchief and a jacket. He covered his bones with an army blanket. And he died.

Oh, how I cried to witness that death! I slumped in a junked car and wailed and mourned as one who has no hope—because I had come to love the Ragman. Every other face had faded in the wonder of this man, and I cherished him, but he died. I sobbed myself to sleep.

I did not know—how could I know?—that I slept through Friday night and Saturday and its night, too.

But then, on Sunday morning, I was wakened by a violence.

Light—pure, hard, demanding light—slammed against my sour face, and I blinked, and I looked, and I saw the last and the first wonder of all. There was the Ragman, folding the blanket most carefully, a scar on his forehead, but alive! And besides that, healthy! There was no sign of sorrow nor of age, and all the rags that he had gathered shined for cleanliness.

Well, then I lowered my head and, trembling for all that I had seen, I myself walked up to the Ragman. I told him my name with shame, for I was a sorry figure next to him. Then I took off my clothes in that place, and I said to him with dear yearning in my voice: "Dress me."

He dressed me. My Lord, he put new rags on me, and I am a wonder beside him. The Ragman, the Ragman, the Christ![3]

Remember earlier how we said if you were going to save a dead person that there were two requirements? First, you have to cure the disease that caused him to die. Second, you would have to give him life. The Ragman, Jesus, did both. He took our disease (sin) and gave us new spiritual life.

The coming of the Lord Jesus Christ for our redemption fulfilled a twofold purpose. First, "the reason the Son of God appeared was to destroy the devil's work" (1 John 3:8). Satan had deceived Eve, and Adam sinned. Consequently they lost their intimacy with God, and Satan became the rebel holder of earthly authority. Jesus affirmed this when He referred to Satan as the "prince of this world" (John 14:30). Because of what Christ accomplished, "the prince of this world now stands condemned" (John 16:11). Jesus "has rescued us from the dominion of darkness and brought us into the kingdom of the Son he loves, in whom we have redemption, the forgiveness of sins" (Colossians 1:13,14).

The second purpose for Jesus' coming was stated by Christ Himself: "I have come that they may have life, and have it to the full" (John 10:10). He was not talking about our present physical life, as if He were going to make it full by giving us an abundance of physical things. He was talking about our spiritual life, our relationship with God. The fullness of life is the fruit of the Spirit—"love, joy, peace, patience, kindness, goodness, faithfulness, gentleness and self-control" (Galatians 5:22,23). He was talking about a redeemed humanity that is fully alive in Christ. What a wonderful gospel!

Salvation Is Past, Present, and Future

Many Christians are easily confused about the concepts of salvation and sanctification because both are presented in the Bible in the past, present, and future verb tenses. Remember that English class you took? Well here is where you put some of that stuff to work. The Bible says we have been saved, we are presently being saved, and we will someday be fully saved. Notice the past tenses in the following verses declaring that in Christ we have been saved:

> Because of his great love for us, God, who is rich in mercy, made us alive with Christ even when we were dead in transgressions—it is by grace you have been saved. . . . For it is by grace you have been saved, through faith—and this not from yourselves, it is the gift of God (Ephesians 2:4,5,8).

> Join with me in suffering for the gospel, by the power of God, who has saved us and called us to a holy life—not because of anything we have done but because of his own purpose and grace (2 Timothy 1:8,9).

> When the kindness and love of God our Savior appeared, he saved us, not because of righteous things we had done, but because of his mercy. He saved us through the washing of rebirth and renewal by the Holy Spirit (Titus 3:4,5).

These verses clearly teach that every child of God has experienced salvation. We have been born again; consequently, we are now spiritually alive. Jesus said, "I am the resurrection and the life. He who believes in me will live, even though he dies; and whoever lives and believes in me will never die" (John 11:25). In other words, because of our belief we are now spiritually alive and will stay alive even when we die physically. We will never die spiritually.

Yet the Bible also tells us we are *presently* "being saved":

> The message of the cross is foolishness to those who are perishing, but to us who are being saved it is the power of God (1 Corinthians 1:18).

> We are to God the aroma of Christ among those who are being saved and those who are perishing (2 Corinthians 2:15).

> My dear friends, as you have always obeyed—not only in my presence, but now much more in my absence—continue to work out your salvation with fear and trembling (Philippians 2:12).

We do not work *for* our salvation, but we are called to work *out* what God has born in us. There is a progressive aspect of sanctification that is similar in concept to the continuing process of salvation. That is, we are "being saved," and we are presently being conformed to the image of God.

Our salvation begins on earth, but it is completed in heaven. That is why the Bible speaks about a future aspect of salvation. Look at the following passages, which teach we shall be saved:

> Since we have now been justified by his blood, how much more shall we be saved from God's wrath (Romans 5:9).

> The hour has come for you to wake up from your slumber, because our salvation is nearer now than when we first believed (Romans 13:11).

> Christ was sacrificed once to take away the sins of many people; and he will appear a second time, not to bear sin, but to bring salvation to those who are waiting for him (Hebrews 9:28).

We have not yet been saved from the wrath that is to come, but we have the assurance that we will be. "Having believed, you were marked in him with a seal, the promised Holy Spirit, who is a deposit guaranteeing our inheritance until the redemption of those who are God's possession—to the praise of his glory" (Ephesians 1:13,14).

Just like salvation, the biblical concept of sanctification carries us all the way from our new birth in Christ to the final perfection of glorification. The Bible clearly speaks of the believer's sanctification as already accomplished, as being accomplished, and, finally, as being completed in the future. These are often referred to as the three tenses of sanctification.

In the next chapter, we are going to identify and explain these three tenses, and then we'll devote the rest of the book to looking at how we as Christians conform to the image of God.

Sold Out

Read

Romans 6:11; Galatians 5:1

Reflect

In what ways are you, like some of those freed slaves, continuing to live in bondage to sin even though you have been spiritually emancipated by Christ's death on the cross?

What are some of the old feelings you currently have that keep you from choosing or recognizing God's truth and freedom?

When did you first become aware of your sinfulness and realize that you were separated from God and needed a personal relationship with Him?

Before becoming a Christian, what did you turn to in your quest for significance?

Respond

Dear heavenly Father, I am so thankful for the grace You have given me. Thank You for saving me in Christ through His death on the cross. Thank You for saving me, and thank You that I am privileged and empowered by You to partner in that process as I work out my salvation. Thank You for removing me from any future judgment. Yours is indeed an amazing grace, and I thank You for it in Jesus' name. Amen.

3

Totally Holy

Some young Christians are happy just knowing they have a ticket to heaven, but a daily relationship with Christ is also part of the adventure. Are you experiencing all that God has for you, or are you happy just watching the parade?

A little boy who lived far out in the country in the late 1800s had reached the age of 12 and had never seen a circus. You can imagine his excitement when one day a poster went up at school announcing that next Saturday a traveling circus was coming to a town nearby. He ran home with the glad news and the question, "Daddy, can I go?" Although the family was poor, the father sensed how important it was to his son. "If you do your chores ahead of time," he said, "I'll see to it that you have the money to go."

Come Saturday morning, the chores were done and the little boy stood by the breakfast table, dressed in his Sunday best. His father reached down into his pocket of his overalls and pulled out a dollar—the most money the little boy had possessed at one time in all his life. The father cautioned him to be careful and then sent him on his way to town.

The boy was so excited his feet hardly seemed to touch the ground all the way. As he neared the outskirts of the village, he noticed people lining the streets. He worked his way through the crowd until he could see what was happening. Lo and behold it was the approaching spectacle of a circus parade!

The parade was the greatest thing he had ever seen. Caged animals snarled as they passed, bands beat their rhythms and sounded shining horns, midgets performed acrobatics while flags and ribbons swirled overhead. Finally, after everything had passed where he was standing, the traditional circus clown, with floppy shoes, baggy pants, and a brightly painted face, brought up the rear. As the clown passed by, the little boy reached into his pocket and took out that precious dollar bill. Handing the money to the clown, the boy turned around and went home.

What had happened? The boy thought he had seen the circus when he had only seen the parade![2]

Every Christian has already been born as a child of God. Next is the process of growth, which calls for us to put off childish things and grow in our relationship with God. Paul said in 1 Corinthians 13:12 that our sanctification is not complete in this lifetime because at this time we don't fully understand all of God's Word and His ways. We see dimly. Right now we are still growing in sanctification—with each stage of growth building upon the previous one—until the time we become like Jesus.

As we study this growth process, it's important for us to understand all three tenses of sanctification so we can see how God has made us holy, continues to make us holy, and ultimately assures us of perfect holiness.

Past-Tense Sanctification

The past tense is often spoken of as *positional* sanctification because it speaks of the holy position or place that the believer has in Christ. The positional truth of who we are in Christ is real truth, and it is the only basis for the *progressive* (present tense) sanctification that follows. Just as the past tense reality of salvation is the basis for the present tense *working out* of our salvation, so also is our position in Christ the basis for our *growth* in Christ. At salvation the believer is set apart or separated unto God and thus participates in God's holiness. Peter explains it this way:

> His divine power has granted [past tense] to us everything pertaining to life and godliness, through the true knowledge of Him who called us by His own glory and excellence. For by these He has granted [past tense] to us His precious and magnificent promises, in order that by them you might become partakers of the divine nature, having escaped [past tense] the corruption that is in the world by lust (2 Peter 1:3,4 NASB).

If you read all that and your brain hurts, look at the explanation in Check It Out!

Past-tense sanctification = Positional sanctification
Our holy position as a child of God = Who we are in Christ

When we hear or read about sanctification, usually it's connected with the present tense, our current Christian growth. But in the Bible the words "sanctification," "sanctify," "saints," and "holy" are most often used in the past tense. For example, when Paul opened his letter to the Corinthian believers, he speaks of them as "those sanctified in Christ Jesus" (1 Corinthians 1:2). Describing the change that took place at salvation, Paul says, "You were washed, you were sanctified, you were justified in the name of the Lord Jesus Christ and by the Spirit of our God" (1 Corinthians 6:19).

At the same time, Paul wrote sternly to the believers at Corinth because they had a ton of problems. So when Paul said they were sanctified, he didn't mean that the Corinthians were living righteously or that they were spiritually grown up. Rather, they were holy because they were in Christ.

When we come to Christ, we are given "an inheritance among all those who are sanctified" (Acts 20:32). In the same way, Jesus said to Paul, "I am sending you to them [the Gentiles] to open their eyes and turn them from darkness to light, and from the power of Satan to God, so that they may receive forgiveness of sins and a place among those who are sanctified by faith in me" (Acts 26:17,18). According to both of these passages, by our faith in Christ we belong to the company of believers who are described as already and yet still being sanctified.

Sinner or Saint?

Do you know what a quisling is? (It's a real word; we didn't make it up.) If somebody calls you a quisling, you should be offended. It's the same as calling someone a "Judas" or a "Benedict Arnold."

Vidkun Quisling was a politician in Norway when Adolph Hitler became the leader of Germany. When the Nazis invaded Norway in 1940, Quisling cooperated with the Germans, and the Germans rewarded him by making him the prime minister of Norway in 1942. He sold out his king and his country to get what he wanted. He also imprisoned and killed people who were still loyal to the king. After Germany lost the war, Quisling was arrested, tried, and executed by a Norwegian court. Ever since that time, quisling has been another word for traitor.

How would you like your name to become a way to call someone a traitor? That would be awful. You don't want to be known as a traitor. You want people to think of you as loyal and trustworthy, right? Of course.[3]

Just like *quisling* identifies a traitor, the title *believer* or *Christian* identifies you as a saint or holy one (check out Romans 1:7; 2 Corinthians 1:1; Philippians 1:1). You may say, "But I've committed so many sins—I'm a sinner." No! When you turned to Jesus, He replaced your old identity with a new one. You have a new title through the holiness of Christ. Being a saint doesn't mean a person is all grown up in terms of character, but it does identify those who are rightly related to God.

In other words, if you come to Christ at the age of six you're obviously not grown up, but you are declared holy.

Believers of any age are called "saints," "holy ones," or "righteous ones" more than 240 times in the King James Version of the Bible. Unbelievers are called "sinners" over 330 times. Clearly, the term *saint* is used in the Bible to refer to the believer, and *sinner* is used in reference to the unbeliever. Although the New Testament gives us plenty of evidence that a believer is capable of sinning, it never clearly identifies the believer as a sinner.

Being a saint is like being God's called or elect ones. Believers are those who are "loved by God and called to be saints" (Romans 1:7; also check out 1 Corinthians 1:2). They are "God's chosen [or elected] people, holy and dearly loved" (Colossians 3:12). They are "chosen…for salvation through sanctification by the Spirit" (2 Thessalonians 2:13 NASB; see also 1 Peter 1:1,2 NASB). God chose and separated them out from the world to be His people.

By the election, and calling of God, we believers are set apart unto Him and belong to the sphere of His holiness. Even though we begin our walk with God as immature babes in Christ, we are without question children of God. We are saints who sin, but in Christ, we have all the resources we need in order not to sin. Paul combined these two concepts of holiness when he wrote to the Ephesians. Addressing them as saints or holy ones in Ephesians 1:1, he goes on in verse 4 to say that God "chose us in him [Christ] . . . to be holy and blameless in his sight." God chose to make these believers holy in Christ, yet His intent was that they would also grow up and mature in their character as they conformed to the image of God.

Made Holy Through Christ

Our positional holiness as believers is solely because we are new creations in Christ. The fact that we put our trust in Jesus' death and resurrection joins us to Christ so that we share in all that He is, including His holiness. As Paul says, "By [God's] doing you are in Christ Jesus, who became to us wisdom from God, and righteousness and sanctification, and redemption" (1 Corinthians 1:30).

Righteousness: Being in a right relationship with God; inner moral conformity of one's character to the character of God.

Sanctification: To make holy, to set apart.

Redemption: To pay a purchase price in order to release another from bondage.

Our holiness in relation to Christ is illustrated by the high priest in the Old Testament, who was a type of Christ's perfect priesthood to come. The Old Testament priest represented the people before God. On his forehead he wore a plate on which was inscribed "Holy to the Lord" (Exodus 28:36). These words proclaimed that he and the people whom he represented—as well as all of the services that he performed on behalf of the people—were completely holy to the Lord. In the same way, Christ represents His people before God. As one who is totally holy (Mark 1:24; Acts 4:27; Revelation 3:7), He represents His people, who are now holy in Him.

When the Old Testament priest came into God's presence representing a people who had sinned, a sacrifice had to be offered. It was only on the basis of atonement to the people's sin that the priest could come before a holy God. So also with Christ. He did not need to make a sacrifice for Himself, but He did in order to bring us into God's holy presence. The writer to the Hebrews emphasizes that our sanctification or relationship to God is based on the perfect sacrifice of Christ for our sins: "We have been made holy through the sacrifice of the body of Jesus Christ once for all. . . . By one sacrifice he has made perfect forever those who are being made holy" (Hebrews 10:10,14). "Jesus also suffered outside the city gate to make the people holy through his own blood" (Hebrews 13:12).

Past-tense sanctification, then, means that we as believers have been brought by God into the sphere of His holiness or purity. We have been brought into fellowship with a holy God. Scripture says that only those who are clean and holy can enter His presence to worship and fellowship with Him. As sinners we could not enter His holy presence. By faith in Christ, who sacrificed Himself to cleanse us of our sins, we are joined to Him and have been invited into the very "holy of holies" of heaven to have fellowship with God. Christ's sacrifice for our sins means that God no longer holds the uncleanness of our sins against us. He now welcomes us into His holy presence.

What About Sin?

Even though we're believers, we still have the ability to sin when we choose to believe Satan's lies and walk according to our old ways. But because of Christ and His sacrifice, our bad choices do not keep us from God's presence: "The death [Christ] died, he died to sin *once for all*" (Romans 6:10, emphasis added). You may ask, "I can accept the truth that Christ has forgiven me for my past sins, but what about my future sins?" Christ died *once for* all—for *all* your sins! Hebrews 10:14 tells us that "by one sacrifice [Christ] has made perfect forever those who are being made holy." Despite the fact that we do sin, God says that "we have confidence to enter the Most Holy Place by the blood of Jesus....And since we have a great priest over the house of God, let us draw near to God with a sincere heart in full assurance of faith, having our hearts sprinkled to cleanse us" (Hebrews 10:19,21,22).

Past-tense sanctification does not mean that we do not sin or have no sin: "If we claim to be without sin, we deceive ourselves and the truth is not in us" (1 John 1:8). It's important to know that "having" sin and "being" sin are two totally different issues. Some people say that separating the two issues denies the doctrine of depravity—the teaching that man is utterly helpless in his sin state. That is not true. The slave was indeed a slave, and there was nothing he could do about it. To say that Christians are still depraved is like the plantation owner telling his slaves that they really aren't free, but they will be someday.

Some people have suggested that telling people who they are in Christ gives them a license to sin. They insist on identifying Christians as sinners saved by grace, but then expect them to act as saints!

This girl's testimony speaks for itself!

Dear Dave,

I grew up in a very strong Christian home with parents who loved me deeply, but set very high expectations for me. Good grades came fairly easy for me. I went to church all the time so everyone pegged me as a good Christian girl. I can't think of anything that drove me more than meeting up to and exceeding those expectations, yet it always seemed like I fell short. No matter how much I excelled, I felt like I could have done more, done better, or been better. Even though it seemed like I had it all together on the outside, I thought of myself as someone who could never quite measure up. These feelings went on for years.

Finally I got so tired one day that I prayed a prayer of desperation. I told God that I quit. If I was ever going to be good enough He was going to have to do it. God slowly began to tear away the things that I had based my self-worth on: grades, gymnastics, my job, and relationships. It seemed like everything that I thought made me me was being torn away. I was forced to ask myself, "Who am I?" I didn't have the answer. I had never felt more worthless and desperate. That's when I made the commitment to do nothing else but seek God.

I came across *Stomping Out the Darkness* and *The Bondage Breaker* and read them. For the first time I started to realize that God loved and accepted me and that I had His approval. I understood that His approval had nothing to do with how good I was. I began to realize that God already sees me as pure and holy and righteous—as a saint. I finally understood that the Christian life isn't doing all the right things so that I would meet up to God's or other people's expectations to avoid feeling guilty. Rather, the Christian life is allowing God to change me into the way He already sees me. For the first time, I was freed from the responsibility of being good enough and freed from the fear of what people think of me.

As I began to understand that God totally loves and accepts me right where I am, I fell in love with Him, and I couldn't help but do what He says. I want to with all my heart. I can't thank you enough for how you have allowed God to use you. My life will never be the same.

Love, Mandy

We believe that telling people who they are in Christ motivates them toward holy living, as it did Mandy. "The

Spirit himself testifies with our spirit that we are God's children" (Romans 8:16). We surely were sinners in desperate need of the grace of God, but "now we are children of God, and what we will be has not yet been made known. But we know that when he appears, we shall be like him, for we shall see him as he is. Everyone who has this hope in him purifies himself, just as he is pure" (1 John 3:2,3).

We were depraved when we were dead in our trespasses and sins. Are we still so depraved? If we are still fundamentally sinners by nature, then shouldn't the dominant pattern of our lives be to live in sin? Is that what saints do? No. John says that those who understand they are children of God and have their hope fixed on Jesus purify themselves. They live according to who they really are—children of God.

Present-Tense Sanctification

God performed an awesome work of grace when He called us out of darkness into His marvelous light and gave us the status of holiness because we were joined with Christ. He did this so that He could carry on His work of making us holy. The process of growing from an unbeliever to Christlikeness is commonly known as present-tense sanctification or *progressive sanctification*. Paul says, "Now that you have been set free from sin and have become slaves to God, the benefit you reap leads to holiness [or sanctification], and the result is eternal life" (Romans 6:22).

The idea of progressive sanctification is the focus of God's work in our lives today. We can define it as God working in the lives of His people, setting them free from sin's bondage and continually renewing them into the image of His own holiness in attitude, character, and actions of life.

Present-tense sanctification = Progressive sanctification

**The process of growth from new believer
to Christlikeness**

**The believer is set apart unto God and thus
participates in God's holiness**

It is important for us to know the difference between *sanctification* and *justification*. In justification, God declares the believer righteous because of the righteousness of Christ, which is accounted to the believer. Justification is the act of a judge. It removes from the sinner the punishment that is deserved because of the guilt of sin. Sanctification, however, deals with the pollution of sin.

When we are joined to Christ through faith, we are clothed in His righteousness so we can stand justified before God. In Christ's righteousness we stand in a right relationship to God in relation to His righteous law. We are also positionally sanctified. We are accepted into God's presence as clean and pure in Christ's holiness. At the same moment we became justified and positionally sanctified, the Spirit of God came into our lives and began the process of transforming our characters through progressive sanctification (Christian growth).

The believer stands justified. We are forgiven and, therefore, not guilty before God. "Having been justified by faith, we have peace with God through our Lord Jesus

Christ" (Romans 5:1 NASB). We were positionally sanctified when we were born again, and we are now being progressively sanctified.

The Bible presents progressive sanctification as a challenge to believers. "Having these promises, beloved, let us cleanse ourselves from all defilement of flesh and spirit, perfecting holiness in the fear of God" (2 Corinthians 7:1 NASB). We are urged to sexual purity because "it is God's will that you should be sanctified" (1 Thessalonians 4:3). Also we are told, "Make every effort to live in peace with all men and to be holy; without holiness no one will see the Lord" (Hebrews 12:14).

Conforming to God's Image

Although the Bible speaks of past-tense sanctification much more frequently than present-tense sanctification, the concept of progressively being made holy is a dominant theme. Terms like *growth, edification, building up, transformation, purification, renewing,* and so on are all related: They refer to the *process* of conforming to the image of God. Let's look at two Bible passages that show this conforming process and see what they reveal about it.

> As you therefore have received Christ Jesus the Lord, so walk in Him, having been firmly rooted and now being built up in Him and established in your faith, just as you were instructed, and overflowing with gratitude (Colossians 2:6,7 NASB).

The phrase "having been firmly rooted . . . in Him" refers to past-tense sanctification. This shows how necessary it is to be firmly committed to Christ first. Many of us are trying to grow on our own efforts, but apart from Christ we can do nothing (John 15:5). We are *saved* by faith, and we are *sanctified* by faith. We cannot grow spiritually on our own.

Every hope we have for living the Christian life comes solely from the grace and life of God. All of Paul's beliefs were rooted in Christ. He wrote to the church in Corinth, "I have sent to you Timothy, who is my beloved and faithful child in the Lord, and he will remind you of my ways which are in Christ, just as I teach everywhere in every church" (1 Corinthians 4:17 NASB). Terms like *in Christ, in Him,* or *in the Beloved* are among the most repeated phrases in the letters (epistles) to the churches. They confirm that we, as new creatures in Christ, are in union with God. We are alive in Christ.

> I write to you, dear children, because your sins have been forgiven on account of his name. I write to you, fathers, because you have known him who is from the beginning. I write to you, young men, because you have overcome the evil one. I write to you, dear children, because you have known the Father. I write to you, fathers, because you have known him who is from the beginning. I write to you, young men, because you are strong, and the word of God lives in you, and you have overcome the evil one (1 John 2:12-14).

In Colossians, Paul says you have to be rooted in Christ before you can be built up in Him, and you have to be built up before you can walk in Him. John uses the pictures of little children, young men, and fathers to describe the process of growing up. Little children are those who have entered into a knowledge of God and have had their sins forgiven. They have overcome the penalty of sin. Fathers, who are more mature, have had a long understanding and knowledge of God. Young men know the

Word of God, are strong, and are characterized as those who have overcome the evil one. In other words, they have overcome the power of sin. But how are we going to grow in the faith if we don't know who we are in Christ and are ignorant of Satan's schemes?

In all the years we've been helping people find their freedom in Christ, the one common reason they were living in defeat was that they didn't know who they were as children of God. They were like the slaves who had heard the news they were free, but were still held hostage by the plantation owner with his double-barrel shotgun. The Bible continually warns against the blinding deceit of the enemy. What he does against the unsaved he continues with us if we let him: "The god of this age has blinded the minds of unbelievers, so that they cannot see the light of the gospel of the glory of Christ" (2 Corinthians 4:4).

The New Man: Becoming Fully Human

Sometimes we think that to be human is to be flawed. But that's not the way it is. Becoming holy is not simply about being conformed to the likeness of God, it is also about being made fully human. Sanctification is the process through which God makes us the whole human beings He created us to be. He is restoring a fallen humanity.

Sin not only distorts people's image of God, it also distorts the people, since to be human as God created us is to exist in the image of God. At salvation, the believer has put on "the new self," "the new man" (Colossians 3:9,10; see also Ephesians 4:24). We will see later that "the new man" can refer both to the individual and the new humanity of which Christ is the head. What is important now is to see that sanctification is also the renewing of our humanity so that we will become who God intended in His original creation.

Sanctification or holiness is often pictured as something somber, which is true in that it involves the death of the old sinful life so that the new life can spring forth. But there's great joy in becoming holy because we're entering into the *fullness* of our humanity: Holiness is not about conforming to the rules of an authoritarian rule-maker; rather, it is about the celebration of our humanity!

Future-Tense Sanctification

In the Bible, the future tense of sanctification is expressed in Paul's explanation of the work and goal of Christ's sacrifice for us: "Christ loved the church and gave himself up for her to make her holy, cleansing her by the washing with water through the word, and to present her to himself as a radiant church, without stain or wrinkle or any other blemish, but holy and blameless" (Ephesians 5:25-27). At salvation, Christ set us apart to Himself that He might finally make us perfectly holy. Paul, in his prayers for other believers, frequently mentioned this ultimate goal:

> May the Lord make your love increase and over-flow for each other and for everyone else, just as ours does for you. May he strengthen your hearts so that you will be blameless and holy in the presence of our God and Father when our Lord Jesus comes with all his holy ones (1 Thessalonians 3:12,13). [Note love's central place in sanctification.]

> May God himself, the God of peace, sanctify you through and through. May your whole spirit, soul and body be kept blameless at the coming of

our Lord Jesus Christ. The one who calls you is faithful and he will do it (1 Thessalonians 5:23,24).

The idea of ultimate sanctification is expressed in other ways as well. Paul said this about God in Philippians 1:6: "He who began a good work in you will carry it on to completion until the day of Christ Jesus [that is, His coming again]." Sharing in the glory of God includes that final perfection of separation from sin and participation in the holiness of God (see Romans 8:30; 2 Thessalonians 2:14). This is most clearly stated in terms of being like Christ. The destiny of believers is to "be conformed to the likeness of [God's] Son" (Romans 8:29) and to "bear the likeness of the man [Jesus] from heaven" (1 Corinthians 15:49).

The Scope of Sanctification

Becoming holy involves the transformation of every part of our being. Like growth in the natural realm, healthy spiritual growth involves growth in every aspect in proper balance. Paul prayed that God would sanctify the Thessalonian believers entirely, or completely. He prayed that their "spirit and soul and body be preserved complete, without blame at the coming of our Lord Jesus Christ" (1 Thessalonians 5:23 NASB).

Sold Out

Read

Hebrews 10:14-22

Reflect

Explain how the word *saint* is used in the New Testament. Check out Romans 1:7 and Philippians 1:1.

We are saints who sin, but we are not identified as sinners. Why?

Explain the difference between "having" sin and "being" sin. Why is knowing this so important?

Why should the fact that you are a child of God motivate you toward a holy life instead of giving you a license to sin?

What do the following verses teach you about justification and positional sanctification: 2 Corinthians 7:1; 1 Thessalonians 4:3; and Hebrews 12:4? Explain.

Respond

Awesome and holy Father, I am in awe that You love me so much that You want to set me apart and make me holy as You are holy. I am so aware of how much I like to sin, yet I am also aware of Your wonderful love and forgiveness. Teach me what it means to live like the child of God that I am and not carry out the desires of the flesh. Thank You that Your work of sanctification—past, present, and future—has been set into motion in my life. Guide me to make the right choices so others might see Christ in me. I want to be like Jesus and be conformed to His image. In Jesus' name I pray, amen.

Now a righteousness from God, apart from law, has been made known, to which the Law and the Prophets testify. This righteousness from God comes through faith in Jesus Christ to all who believe.

—Romans 3:21,22

He who would know holiness must understand sin.[1]

—*Horatius Bonar*

A Radically Changed Relationship

Sin is the only thing that can separate us from God, but God is so loving that He wants to rescue us from sin's terrible effects. Some people try to run from God because they think He wants to punish them. Have you felt that way? What God really wants to do is save lives, just like the police in this news story. God wants us to grow in Him.

Thousands of cars are stolen every year in California, but in 1981, there was one car theft that made all the local papers and was the lead story on the evening news. The police had issued an all-points bulletin to find the missing car and to make contact with the people who stole it.

Why was this car theft getting so much attention?

The owner of the car had informed the police that on the front seat of the car was a box of crackers laced with a deadly poison. The car owner had planned to use the crackers as rat bait. So the police were desperately trying to find the thief—not to punish him, but to save his life. They were afraid he would eat one of the crackers.[2]

The True Nature of Sin

Growth in the Christian life is totally dependent upon God's graceful presence in our lives; so, to grow, we must be rightly related to Him. But before we receive Christ, sin separates us from the righteous and holy God. As the prophet Isaiah said, "Your iniquities have separated you from your God" (Isaiah 59:2). Our natural state is described by Paul as dead in transgressions and sins and, as a consequence, separated from the life of God (see Ephesians 2:1; 4:18).

Imagine that everyone in the United States was told that they have to either swim to Hawaii or die. There would be all kinds of people with different shapes and sizes lined up on the coast of California ready to give it their best effort.

There would be the 500-pound man who can barely walk across the room without getting out of breath. As he begins to walk out into the water, a big wave knocks him over and he can't get up, so he gargles salt water and drowns.

Then there would be the middle-aged guy who used to be a great swimmer. He begins to swim, but it isn't long before he begins to get tired. He practices the dead man's float he learned in Boy Scouts. He tries to keep going, but eventually he gives out. He too gargles salt water and drowns.

Then there would be the girl from the high school swim team. She has been swimming every day of her life for the past 10 years. She is in excellent physical condition. She begins to swim slowly and steadily—one mile, two miles, ten miles—but she begins to get cramps in her tired muscles. She can't go on. She too gargles salt water and drowns.

Then there would be a marathon swimmer, like the guys who swim the English Channel. He would start out swimming strong and steady. He passes the 10-mile mark, the 20-mile mark and even the 50-mile mark, but eventually he too begins to wear down. The waves take their toll and he finally gargles salt water and drowns.

Although some swimmers are much better than others, there is not a single swimmer, no matter how great, who can swim all the way to Hawaii.

Just as the best swimmer can't swim all the way to Hawaii from California, even the best person in the world can't get into heaven on the basis of his or her good works. It is only God's grace that makes the journey to heaven possible.[3]

Before a person can grow, he or she must have a relationship with God. This requires dealing with the reality of sin. The Bible says that all people are naturally sinners: "All have sinned and fall short of the glory of God" (Romans 3:23). All are under sin, a power that dominates their lives and brings guilt and condemnation before God as well as self (Romans 3:9; Galatians 3:22).

There are two harmful ways people view sin that we need to look at.

The first view is held by people who seem to have no moral conscience or awareness of their own sin. "Were they ashamed because of the abomination they have done? They were not even ashamed at all; they did not even know how to blush" (Jeremiah 6:15 NASB). These kind of people obviously have no relationship with God.

What's really sad, however, is the other view of sin which is held by those who have a relationship with God. Even though they are totally justified in the eyes of God, these believers are overwhelmed by their sins and cannot seem to accept God's forgiveness. They keep trying to earn God's favor by doing good, and they get trapped in the bondage of legalism. They are plagued with condemning thoughts by Satan (Revelation 12:10) and question their salvation. Even though Scripture teaches "there is now no condemnation for those who are in Christ Jesus" (Romans 8:1), they can't seem to rest in that truth. There are a few other reasons we have a difficult time grasping the true nature of sin.

First, we have always been personally involved in sin and live in an environment conditioned by sin. It is difficult, if not impossible, for us to fully grasp the difference between living in sin and living in righteousness because we have never experienced perfect righteousness and holiness. Our understanding is also limited by our brain-power; we simply cannot understand sin in its full depth.

Second, our understanding is skewed because of our own sinfulness. Most people tend to minimize or think less of their sin than they should in order to excuse themselves or justify their actions. This can be demonstrated by the excuses found on some actual accident forms that turn up at insurance companies as people tried to lessen their responsibility:

> "The pedestrian had no idea which direction to go, so I ran over him."

> "An invisible car came out of nowhere, struck my vehicle, and vanished."

> "The guy was all over the road. I had to swerve a number of times before I hit him."

> "A pedestrian hit me and went under my car."[4]

These reports reveal that people would rather rationalize sin than admit to a mistake. We're sure you've heard people say, "Well everybody does it!" or "I'm not as bad as that person over there." These kinds of comparisons don't work with God.

Third, our awareness of what is sinful can easily grow dull with tolerance and exposure to it. For instance, the profanity and explicit sex commonly accepted in today's television shows and movies would never have been tolerated 40 years ago.

Fourth, no human has yet experienced the full weight of sin's consequences. We don't take sin very seriously, and we usually don't count the cost until later.

> Several years ago, newspapers carried a story about an elderly lady who lived in the Big Cypress Swamp in South Florida. Her home was an old shack located by a small pond. Every day the lady went to the pond to draw water. In the pond lived an alligator. Despite the danger, the lady allowed this alligator to live in the pond for years. It seemed tame. She didn't bother the gator, and the gator didn't bother her.

However, one day while she was drawing water from the pond, the alligator swam under the water and then plunged up, grabbing the old woman's hand with his mighty jaws. She tried to pull her hand out of his mouth, but the gator ripped it off. Bleeding and terribly stunned, the old woman called for help. The paramedics came, and she received medical attention.

The next day the park ranger came and killed the gator. When they cut it open they found the old woman's hand.

The park ranger told reporters that "alligators are most dangerous when they lose their fear of humans. By allowing an alligator to remain in your pond, you unknowingly give it the courage to attack. The lady still lives in the swamp, but there are no alligators in her pond."[5]

So many times we are like the old woman in the news story. We think we can keep sin in our lives and not suffer the consequences. We think because it hasn't bitten us today that we are safe tomorrow. If we all got what we deserved right now, we would immediately be cast into hell. If we only knew the damage caused by the sins we thought we got away with, we would cover our faces in shame. Secret sin on earth is open scandal in heaven. And despite God's occasional judgments upon sinful humanity throughout history, the full consequences of sin have not yet been poured out on anyone.

The Bible shows how terrible and powerful sin is. Sin's strength is greater than any human effort. It reigns as king over fallen mankind and leads people to their deaths (Romans 5:21). The problem of sin and its power over our lives cannot be overcome by any natural means—that would fail just like the swimmers trying to make it from California to Hawaii. Sin is not mere ignorance that can be overcome by education. Sin is more than bad habits that can be overcome by the practice of moral disciplines. It is more than a twisted personality that can be overcome with the help of psychology. Sin is a power that enslaves us. Paul's cry represents the reality of all people under sin's domination: "What a wretched man I am! Who will rescue me from this body of death? Thanks be to God—through Jesus Christ our Lord!" (Romans 7:24,25). Only the superior power of God in Christ can redeem us from the reigning power of sin.

A Relationship Broken by Sin

At creation, Adam and Eve had a relationship with God. In this relationship, Adam and Eve were designed to grow in every way to full maturity as human beings. Sin broke this relationship and assumed the place of God. The original sin of Adam and Eve reveals what sin is. The temptation (as is every temptation) was an attempt by Satan to get Adam and Eve to use their free will independent of God. They disobeyed God by eating the forbidden fruit of the tree of the knowledge of good and evil. The real essence of sin is seen in Satan's words, "Your eyes will be opened, and you will be like God, knowing good and evil" (Genesis 3:5).

Every manifestation of sin, from bad attitudes to hurtful actions, stems from the one root of all sin— the desire to play god.

To have knowledge of good and evil means to be the one who decides what is good or evil and what is true or untrue. When Adam and Eve chose to eat the forbidden fruit, they were saying, "We reject God as the one who determines what is right or wrong. We'll decide for ourselves what is good for us, and we think that eating this fruit is, in fact, for our good." They played right into the hands of the devil, who is a deceiver and the father of lies.

In a distorted way, Satan was right when he said "You will be like God, knowing good and evil." Adam and Eve acted like gods in determining for themselves what was right. But what they determined was wrong. Rather than embracing the truth that would preserve their freedom, they believed a lie that led to death and bondage to sin. All sin is the inevitable consequence of rebellion toward God: "Everything that does not come from faith is sin" (Romans 14:23).

Since God is the only source of life, living apart from God can only mean death. Being separated from God, Adam and Eve, and all their descendants (that's us), had to find their own means to survive. Ultimately, every act of sin stems from people's attempts to meet their own needs, establish their own identities, receive acceptance from others, attain personal security, and find significance (without God). Acting like gods, we struggle to gain these things through physical appearance, performance, and status.

A Change in Our Legal Relationship

Raynald III was a fourteenth-century duke in what is now Belgium. He was grossly overweight. When he was captured by his younger brother during a revolt, he was imprisoned in a room that was built around him. The room had no bars on the windows and no lock on the door. The only problem was that the door was slightly smaller than normal size. Due to his size, Raynald III could not squeeze through the opening and set himself free.

Yet there was still hope. If he could lose enough weight, he could go free. And not only could he go free, but his brother offered to restore his title and all his wealth as soon as he left the room.

The reason the younger brother made this offer was because he knew his brother's weakness. Raynald loved to eat more than anything in the world. Each day the younger brother had a variety of delicious foods sent to Raynald's room. You can guess what happened. Instead of growing thinner, he grew fatter. He was a prisoner not of locks, bars or iron gates, but of his own appetite.[6]

Raynald's sin cut him off from the world and the possibility of any meaningful relationships. In the Bible, all people are said to be "shut up," "imprisoned," or "under sin," which means they are under the power and condemnation of sin (see Galatians 3:22).

Sin defies God's laws and brings a break in fellowship with Him. We might say that sin is a breaking of our legal relationship with God. We are guilty of breaking His laws and, therefore, no longer stand in a right relationship with Him.

As a result, the sinner stands under God's punishment as a lawbreaker: "Cursed is everyone who does not continue to do everything written in the Book of the Law" (Galatians 3:10). Although Paul's statement contains a specific reference to the Old Testament Law of Moses, it applies to *all* people in relation to God's moral laws.

In Romans 3:19, Paul wrote, "We know that whatever the law says, it says to those who are under the law, so that every mouth may be silenced and the whole world held accountable to God." The word *accountable* in that verse "describes an accused person who cannot say anything to defend himself because he has no more ways to refute the charge against him and stop the judgment from being handed down."[7]

Sin breaks our legal relationship with God, causing us to stand guilty and under the condemnation of God. Sin also breaks our personal moral relationship with Him, causing our nature to be impure and at odds with God's holiness and purity.

Another effect of sin is that it not only brings guilt before God, it also brings pollution and corruption into the life of the sinner. It makes what is pure and holy defiled and impure. It takes what is ordered and beautiful and makes it disfigured and ugly. The Bible teaches that we cannot have fellowship with God unless we are pure and clean. Paul asks, "What fellowship has light with darkness?" (2 Corinthians 6:14 NASB).

Only people with clean hands and a pure heart can stand in God's holy presence (see Psalm 24:3,4). David asked for a pure heart so that he could live in the presence of God and His Holy Spirit (Psalm 51:10,11). Isaiah's uncleanness needed the cleansing touch of an angel's burning coal (Isaiah 6:5-7). James commands, "Come near to God and he will come near to you." But then he goes on to add what is necessary: "Wash your hands . . . and purify your hearts . . ." (James 4:8). It is the pure in heart who will see God, who will experience intimate fellowship with Him (Matthew 5:8).

Restoring the Relationship

Let's suppose that a friend you personally taught how to drive suddenly turns on you. You let him use your car, bought the gas, spent hours showing him how to drive and teaching him traffic laws. Suddenly, without cause, he turns on you. One day he takes your car for a joy ride without asking. To make matters worse, your next door neighbor reported your car as stolen, and the police are now after your friend. In an attempt to escape from the police, your friend leads them on a high-speed chase through the city, hitting a number of parked cars. Finally, he totals your car. Your friend is brought before the judge. You have the right to prosecute, and even if you drop the charges he will still have to pay for the other cars he damaged. Would you be willing to drop the charges and pay for the other cars to free your friend? Our most natural response would be to say, "That self-seeking traitor got what he deserved. Let him rot in jail." We most likely wouldn't be willing to take the initiative to win him back at any great cost—especially if we had to sacrifice our own money.

No illustration can come close to capturing the incredible love that God demonstrates when He takes the initiative to restore a person's relationship with Himself, especially when the fault lies entirely with the sin of the person. "God so loved the world that he gave his one and only Son, that whoever believes in him shall not perish but have eternal life" (John 3:16). It was *God* who sought Adam and Eve in the Garden of Eden after they sinned. He always takes the initiative.

We are not going to be saved by how we behave,
but by how we believe.

We, however, want to hide from God or pretend that He doesn't exist as we seek to cover up our guilt and shame. A proper understanding of our restored relationship with God is absolutely essential to our spiritual growth. We cannot begin to grow unless the relationship is restored with the Author of life. This happens through "justification." *Justification*, in this sense, is a judge's pronouncement of a person's right-standing before the law. When a judge condemns someone, he does not *make* the person a sinner, he simply *declares* that such is the case. In our justification, God is *declaring* that we are in right-standing before His law. The punishment due our sins has been removed. This change of legal relationship is totally a gift from God because of Christ's work for us. Romans 3:21-26 makes clear this truth:

> Now a righteousness from God, apart from law, has been made known, to which the Law and the Prophets testify. This righteousness from God comes through faith in Jesus Christ to all who believe. There is no difference, for all have sinned and fall short of the glory of God, and are justified freely by his grace through the redemption that came by Christ Jesus. God presented him as a sacrifice of atonement, through faith in his blood. He

did this to demonstrate his justice, because in his forbearance he had left the sins committed beforehand unpunished—he did it to demonstrate his justice at the present time, so as to be just and the one who justifies those who have faith in Jesus.

Several truths in this passage are important to catch. First, the righteousness which provides the basis for God to declare us right is *His* and not ours. It is a "righteousness from God, apart from law," or apart from our keeping His law. We are not going to be saved by how we behave, but by how we believe.

"Propitiation" means God's righteous demands or anger have been satisfied through Christ's death on the cross.

Second, the righteousness made available to us is the righteousness that is in Christ Jesus. This righteousness is based on Christ's work for us. Verse 24 says that our justification is "through the redemption that came by Christ Jesus." How it came by Christ in redemption is further explained: He was "a sacrifice of atonement" or, more literally, a "propitiation" (verse 25, NASB). He was a sacrifice that satisfied God's wrath and judgment against the breakers of His moral law—us. Paul says in Galatians 3:13, "Christ redeemed us from the curse of the law by becoming a curse for us."

The forgiveness of our sins through Christ's payment of the penalty is not all that's necessary for God to declare us righteous. Christ forgave us by taking the consequences of our sins upon Himself. Forgiveness *erases* the penalty of sin, but it doesn't provide us with a positive righteousness by which God can declare us righteous. Our need for true righteousness is supplied by Christ's total obedience to God. We know this because Paul says, "Through the obedience of the one man the many will be made righteous" (Romans 5:19).[8] Because of God's work, we are "in Christ Jesus, who has become for us wisdom from God—that is, our righteousness, holiness and redemption" (1 Corinthians 1:30). This last statement helps us understand the whole situation: Christ is our righteousness because we are in Him. We are, as Isaiah said, "clothed . . . with garments of salvation and arrayed . . . in a robe of righteousness" (Isaiah 61:10). This aspect of our justification, then, is supplied by the imputing or reckoning of Christ's righteousness to us so that in Him we stand perfectly righteous before God.

Third, because the forgiveness and righteousness we receive is all from God, our justification is totally a matter of God's grace. We are "justified freely [as a gift] by his grace" (Romans 3:24).

Finally, our justification or right-standing before God comes to us solely through faith in Jesus Christ: "This righteousness from God comes through faith in Jesus Christ to all who believe" (verse 22). God justifies those who have faith in Jesus. That justification is by faith alone should be easy to understand because the person under sin cannot provide his own righteousness by which he might be justified. Forgiveness of sins and a positive righteousness in Christ are God's gracious gift to which the sinner can add nothing, and nothing more is needed. All that is required on the part of sinful humanity is to receive the free gift of eternal life, gratefully accept God's forgiveness, and believe that we are fully justified before God by virtue of the blood of the Lord Jesus Christ.

The Results of Our Restoration

Paul writes, "Since *we have been justified* through faith, we have peace with God through our Lord Jesus Christ, through whom we have gained access by faith into this grace in which we now stand. And we rejoice in the hope of the glory of God" (Romans 5:1-3, emphasis added). These verses point to the fruits of justification, which provide the basis for growth in the Christian life.

Note Paul's use of the past tense: "We *have been* justified." Too many Christians live under false condemnation. They walk on eggshells hoping God won't find out what they are really like. When they make some little mistake in life they think, *I'm going to get it now!* They live in fearful anticipation that the hammer of God is going to fall any minute. Listen you guys, the hammer has already fallen. It fell on Christ. That is the good news. God loves you. "There is no fear in love, but perfect love casts out fear, because fear involves punishment, and the one who fears is not perfected in love" (1 John 4:18 NASB).

Peace with God

Because we have been justified, we have peace with God. Before justification we were enemies, alienated from God (see Romans 5:9,10). Now we stand in right relationship to Him. We are reconciled and saved from His wrath. And now *no one* can condemn us (see Romans 8:33,34).

The concepts of peace and righteousness are often linked together in the Bible (see Psalm 72:3 NASB; 85:10; Isaiah 9:6,7; 32:17; 48:18; 60:17). God cannot make peace with sin. But through His gracious gift we stand justified in Christ, clothed with His righteousness. Therefore we have peace with God.

If you were a sinner in the hands of an angry God, would you approach Him? Most people probably wouldn't! The Israelites were afraid when they saw God as a consuming fire on Mount Horeb. The occasion was the giving of the Mosaic Law. We see their response in Exodus 20:18-21:

> When the people saw the thunder and lightning and heard the trumpet and saw the mountain in smoke, they trembled with fear. They stayed at a distance and said to Moses, "Speak to us yourself and we will listen. But do not have God speak to us or we will die."
>
> Moses said to the people, "Do not be afraid. God has come to test you, so that the fear of God will be with you to keep from sinning."
>
> The people remained at a distance, while Moses approached the thick darkness where God was.

The Israelites were afraid because they wanted to avoid punishment. They preferred a secondhand experience with God. That, unfortunately, is true of many young Christians today. They go to youth group or church just often enough to get God off their backs. Once they have their "fire insurance" against hell, that's enough. Some people feel totally unable to approach God, so they ask or expect their youth pastor or others to do it for them, just as the Israelites asked Moses to intercede for them. But we can't have a second-hand relationship with God. A youth pastor is not a mediator. There is only one mediator between God and man, and that is Jesus Christ (1 Timothy 2:5).

We as Christians do not need to live under any sense of condemnation, nor do we need to ask other people to intercede before God on our behalf. Although there is a place for possessing a proper fear of God's discipline if we persist in sin, the greatest motivation to living a holy life should not be the threat of hurt. Rather, we should be compelled to draw near to Him out of love—a love borne out of gratitude for what He has done for us. We can run to Him knowing that He is our safe house.

Access to God

Justification through the gift of God's righteousness in Christ brings the privilege of access into His presence. Before Christ made God's righteousness available to mankind through His work, only the high priest—on the basis of animal sacrifice—had access into the presence of God in the Holy of Holies of the temple. But now, because of Christ's sacrifice, all believers in Him can come directly into God's holy presence.

We will find unconditional love and acceptance when we come into His presence. Hebrews 4:16 says "Let us then approach the throne of grace with confidence, so that we may receive mercy and find grace to help us in our time of need."

A Change in Our Moral Relationship

We have seen that God is holy and pure and only those who are holy and pure can enjoy fellowship and intimacy with Him. Because fallen humanity is by nature unclean and unholy, a change is required. The change that allows us to have fellowship with a holy God is most often called positional sanctification. As we saw in chapter two, this refers to our holy position in Christ. Even as the believer in Christ is clothed with His righteousness, so also is he clothed with Christ's holiness. The believer is declared righteous not because of his own holiness but because of the holiness of Christ.

Positional sanctification is not fictional; a *real* change has taken place in relationship to our holiness. By the grace of God and His calling of us to Himself, we have been separated from sin and set apart for Him. As part of this *reality*, sin's power over us has been broken. We are to consider ourselves alive in Christ and dead to sin (Romans 6:11). Believing it doesn't make it true; we are to believe it because it *is* true. Because we are alive in Christ, sin no longer has any power over us. We belong to a new master and are legally free from the bondage of sin.

> Back in the 1800s, a young Englishman traveled to California in search of gold. After several months of prospecting he struck it rich. On his way home he stopped in New Orleans. Not long into his visit, he came upon a crowd of people all looking in the same direction. Approaching the crowd, he realized that they had gathered for a slave auction. Slavery had been outlawed in England for years, so this young man's curiosity drew him to watch as a person became someone else's property. He heard "sold" just as he joined the crowd. A middle-aged black man was taken away.
>
> Next a beautiful young black girl was pushed up on the platform and made to walk around so everyone could see her. The bidding began.
>
> Soon the bids surpassed what most slaveholders would pay. As the bidding continued higher and higher, it was apparent that two slave owners wanted her. The miner stood silent as anger welled up inside of him.

Finally, one man bid a price that was beyond the reach of the other. The girl looked down. The auctioneer called out, "Going once! Going twice!"

Just before the final call, the miner called out a price that was exactly twice the previous bid. An amount that exceeded the worth of any man. The crowd laughed, thinking the miner was only joking. The auctioneer motioned to the miner to come forward and show his money. The miner opened up the bag of gold he had brought for the trip. The auctioneer shook his head in disbelief as he waved the girl over to him.

The girl walked down the steps of the platform until she was eye to eye with the miner. She spat straight in his face and said through clenched teeth, "I hate you!" The miner, without a word, wiped his face, paid the auctioneer, took the girl by the hand, and walked away from the still-laughing crowd.

He seemed to be looking for something in particular as they walked up one street and down the other. Finally they stopped in front of some sort of store, though the slave girl did not know what kind of a store it was. She waited outside as the dirty-faced miner went inside and started talking to an elderly man. She couldn't make out what they were talking about. At one point voices got louder, and she overheard the store clerk say, "But it's the law! It's the law!" Peering in, she saw the miner pull out his bag of gold and pour what was left on the table.

With what seemed like a look of disgust, the clerk picked up the gold and went into a back room. He came out with a piece of paper and both he and the miner signed it.

The young girl looked away as the miner came out the door. Stretching out his hand, he said to the girl, "Here are your manumission papers. You are free."

The girl didn't look up.

He tried again. "Here. These are papers that say you are free. Take them."

"I hate you!" the girl said, refusing to look up. "Why do you make fun of me?"

"No, listen," he pleaded. "These are your freedom papers. You are a free person."

The girl looked at the papers then looked at him, and looked at the papers again. "You just bought me...and now you're setting me free?"

"That's why I bought you. I bought you to set you free."

The beautiful girl fell to her knees in front of the miner, tears streaming down her face.

"You bought me to set me free! You bought me to set me free!" she said over and over.

The miner said nothing.

Clutching his muddy boots the girl looked up at the miner and said, "All I want to do is to serve you—because you bought me to set me free."[9]

All of us were once slaves to sin and death, but Christ bought us to set us free. He didn't purchase us with gold; He bought us with His own life!

Because of Christ's death and resurrection, we are new creations in Christ. We are no longer in Adam; we are in Christ. We can say with Paul, "I have been crucified with Christ and I no longer live, but Christ lives in me. The life I live in the body, I live by faith in the Son of God, who loved me and gave himself for me" (Galatians 2:20). This definite or definitive sanctification, which takes place at the time of our salvation in Christ, is the point from which we now grow in progressive or experiential sanctification. Progressive sanctification begins with the realization of our new position and the definitive change of relationship to God and sin in actual-life experiences. Listen to what Paul says:

> You are all sons of God through faith in Christ
> Jesus, for all of you who were baptized into Christ

have clothed yourselves with Christ. There is neither Jew nor Greek, slave nor free, male nor female, for you are all one in Christ Jesus. If you belong to Christ, then you are Abraham's seed, and heirs according to the promise. . . . Because you are sons, God sent the Spirit of his Son into our hearts, the Spirit who calls out, "Abba, Father." So you are no longer a slave, but a son; and since you are a son, God has made you also an heir (Galatians 3:26-29; 4:6,7).

Our justification through Christ's righteous obedience removes the condemnation from the guilt of sin, and our sanctification in Christ's holiness makes it possible to walk in fellowship with God. Prior to salvation, we could not fellowship with God because light cannot fellowship with darkness. Formerly we were "darkness," but now we are "light in the Lord" (Ephesians 5:8) and can have fellowship with a holy God. We can draw near to Him and enter the most holy place of His presence with confidence because of our sanctification in the holiness of Christ (Hebrews 10:19,22).

Recognizing Our New Identity

Peace and acceptance with God are what makes it possible for us to experience *practical* sanctification. True spiritual growth happens only when we have a personal relationship with God. Because we as Christians are no longer enemies with God and are free from the fear of His condemning judgment, we can enjoy a relationship in which we are conformed more and more into His likeness.

This growth cannot take place, however, if we still see ourselves as slaves of sin and we live under fear of condemnation. Only as we see ourselves as sons and daughters of God can we really grow in holiness (see Romans 8:15).

Only as we are free from the task of trying to gain a relationship with God by our own righteousness will we be free to put on His righteousness and holiness for our growth.

Jesus chose His disciples that they might bear fruit (John 15:16). Notice that this challenge came to them after they were *already* attached to the vine. They were to grow *from* the position they had in Christ, not grow by trying to attain position. They were to grow from a position of "cleanness" ("you are already clean"—John 15:3). They did not have to work to become clean.

Jesus taught what sanctification was all about when He said to love God and our neighbor (Matthew 22:37-40). But we cannot love unless we recognize and receive God's love for us. "We love because he first loved us" (1 John 4:19) and because "Christ's love compels us" (2 Corinthians 5:14).

Finally, Paul says that we are "transformed into [Christ's] likeness" as our faces are turned toward the Lord and as we reflect His glory (2 Corinthians 3:18). But we will turn our faces toward Him only if we are friends. And, through Christ, we *are* friends: "I no longer call you servants, because a servant does not know his master's business. Instead, I have called you friends" (John 15:15).

As children of God, we have the assurance that God will supply all our needs "according to His riches in glory in Christ Jesus" (Philippians 4:19 NASB). The most critical needs that all of us have, which are wonderfully met in Christ, are the "being" needs. They are life itself, identity, acceptance, security, and significance. Read through the following scriptural list which was taken from the *Stomping Out the Darkness* youth conference workbook, and recognize who you are in Christ.

IN CHRIST

I AM ACCEPTED

John 1:12:	I am God's child.
John 15:15:	I am Jesus' chosen friend.
Romans 5:1:	I am holy and acceptable to God (justified).
1 Corinthians 6:17:	I am united with the Lord and am one spirit with Him.
1 Corinthians 6:19,20:	I have been bought with a price. I belong to God.
1 Corinthians 12:27:	I am part of Christ's body, part of His family.
Ephesians 1:1:	I am a saint, a holy one.
Ephesians 1:5:	I have been adopted as God's child.
Colossians 1:14:	I have been bought back (redeemed) and forgiven of all my sins.
Colossians 2:10:	I am complete in Christ.

I AM SECURE

Romans 8:1,2:	I am free from punishment.
Romans 8:28:	I know all things work together for good.
Romans 8:31ff.:	I am free from any condemning charges against me.
Romans 8:35ff.:	I cannot be separated from the love of God.

Colossians 3:3:   I am hidden with Christ in God.

Philippians 1:6:   I am sure that the good work God has started in me will be finished.

Philippians 3:20:   I am a citizen of heaven with the rest of God's family.

Hebrews 4:16:   I can find grace and mercy in times of need.

1 John 5:18:   I am born of God, and the evil one cannot touch me.

I AM SIGNIFICANT

Matthew 5:13:   I am the salt and light for everyone around me.

John 15:1,5:   I am a part of the true vine, joined to Christ and able to produce lots of fruit.

John 15:16:   I have been handpicked by Jesus to bear fruit.

Acts 1:8:   I am a spirit-empowered witness for Christ.

1 Corinthians 3:16:   I am a temple where the Holy Spirit lives.

2 Corinthians 5:17ff.:   I am at peace with God, and He has given me the work of making peace between Himself and other people.

2 Corinthians 6:1:   I am God's coworker.

Ephesians 2:6:   I am seated with Christ in heaven.

Ephesians 2:10:   I am God's building project—His handiwork—created to do His work.

Philippians 4:13: I can do all things through Christ who gives me strength.

Sold Out

Read

Romans 3:21-26

Reflect

Have you ever felt overwhelmed with your sin, unable to accept God's forgiveness? What did you do?

What sin do you tend to make excuses for rather than confess? What does looking at the cross of Christ tell you about the true nature of sin? Explain.

What are some consequences of sin? (Check out Galatians 3:10,22; 2 Corinthians 6:14.)

According to Romans 3:22,26,30, what must we do to receive a right-standing before God (justification)?

Review the "In Christ" statements on pages 87-89. Memorize the one that means the most to you.

Respond

Lord, I must admit to You that I really don't know how terrible and awful sin is. I treat it like it is no big deal; I act like sin doesn't hurt me, and I forget how much it hurts You. I am awestruck that You loved me so much that You sent Your only Son to die for my sins. Thank You, Lord! You accept me as Your child and treat me like I never committed a sin. Teach me how to live the way Jesus lived. Help me live for Your kingdom and for others, rather than just living for myself. I want more than anything else in life to resemble Jesus. I pray this in Jesus' awesome name, amen.

*In my inner being
I delight in God's law.*

—ROMANS 7:22

The point is that the things most highly treasured occupy the "heart," the center of the personality.... And thus the most cherished treasure subtly but infallibly controls the whole person's directions and values.[1]

—*D.A. Carson*

A New You with a New Heart

Have you ever seen an ornamental orange tree? They are pretty to look at, but not fit to eat. Why do people have trees that look good but don't bear real fruit? Well, since the ornamental trees have good hardy stock and need very little care, cities put them in parks and line the streets with them. Ornamental orange trees are also used as root stock: After the tree grows to a certain height, the top is cut off and a new life (such as a navel orange tree) is grafted in. Everything that grows above the graft takes on the nature of the sweet navel orange tree; everything below the graft is still physically a hardy ornamental tree. The end result is a tree with solid roots in the earth that produces great-tasting oranges. Although the analogy is a little different than the picture Jesus gave of the vine in John, we're sure you'll see the similarities:

> I am the Real Vine and my Father is the Farmer. He cuts off every branch of me that doesn't bear grapes. And every branch that is grape-bearing he prunes back so it will bear even more. You are already pruned back by the message I have spoken.
>
> Live in me. Make your home in me just as I do in you. In the same way that a branch can't bear fruit by itself but only by being joined to the vine, you can't bear fruit unless you are joined with me.
>
> I am the Vine, you are the branches. When you're joined with me and I with you, the relation intimate and organic, the harvest is sure to be abundant (John 15:1-5 THE MESSAGE).

Spiritual growth in the Christian life requires a relationship with God, who is the foundation of spiritual life. So unless there is a root of life within the believer, growth is impossible.

The New Birth

Adam and Eve were born both physically and spiritually alive. Because of sin, they died spiritually. They were separated from God. From that time on, everyone who has come into this world has been born physically alive but spiritually dead (Ephesians 2:1). In that state, man is completely unable to understand the things of God (1 Corinthians 2:14). Like an ornamental orange tree, he may look good, but the fruit he bears is bitter. All it's good for is to be dropped on the ground and, sadly, bring forth more bitter plants. Every person is basically made up of the body (physical nature) and the inner person (spiritual nature). According to the Bible, the center of the person is the heart, which represents the capacity to think, feel, and choose. In our natural state, "the heart is deceitful above all things and beyond cure" (Jeremiah 17:9). It is deceitful because it was born separated from God with a natural tendency to be its own god. It has been conditioned from the time of birth by the deceitfulness of a fallen world rather than by the truth of God's Word. According to Proverbs 4:23, the heart is the "wellspring of life," in which wickedness must not be allowed to take root. (That is why we are to forgive from the heart and not allow bitterness to spring up.) Although no two-dimensional diagram is adequate to show who we are, the following is a functional depiction of the natural man:

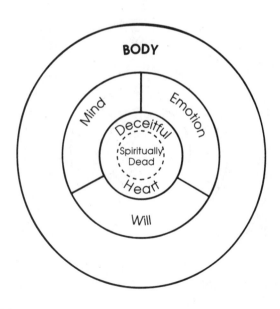

One of the greatest prophecies concerning our salvation is given in Ezekiel 36:26: "I will give you a new heart and put a new spirit in you; I will remove from you your heart of stone and give you a heart of flesh." In the new covenant (which every Christian lives under), God says, "I will put my laws in their hearts" (Hebrews 10:16). Jesus came that we might have life, and the believer receives that spiritual life at the moment of salvation: "To all who received him, to those who believed in his name, he gave the right to become children of God" (John 1:12). In other words, all ornamental orange trees that choose to put their trust in Christ will become navel orange trees.

The moment you were grafted into the vine, you were set apart (sanctified) as a child of God. "You're already clean" (John 15:3), and you will continue to be sanctified as Christ prunes you so that you will grow and bear fruit. You are now alive in Christ, who is the foundation and

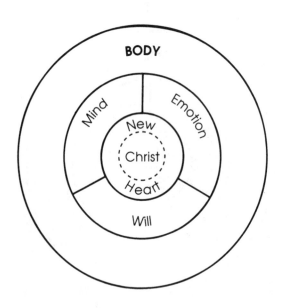

source for spiritual growth. The change from the old state of being spiritually dead as a result of sin is so great that salvation is described as a new birth. You are described as a new creation with a new life that has new desires and a new direction. The diagram on the previous page depicts every born-again child of God.

Our newness as believers in Christ is expressed in several meaningful ways in the Bible. God has given us "new birth into a living hope through the resurrection of Jesus Christ from the dead" (1 Peter 1:3). We have been "born again . . . through the living and enduring word of God" (1 Peter 1:23; see also James 1:18). New Christians are called "newborn babies" and challenged to "crave pure spiritual milk, so that by it you may grow up in your salvation" (1 Peter 2:2).

A great example of the new birth of the believer is found in Jesus' teaching to Nicodemus: "I tell you the truth, no one can enter the kingdom of God unless he is born [again]. . . .You must be born again" (John 3:5,7). It is a birth from heaven by the Spirit (verse 8). This new birth of the believer is also described as a *regeneration*; we have been saved "by the washing of regeneration" (Titus 3:5 NASB). The idea in regeneration is "a new beginning."

> In Louisiana, there was a trial that held the attention of the entire state. The year was 1982, and a man was condemned to die for the murder of a family. As he sat on death row, his attorneys frantically tried to secure a pardon for their client. They used just about every means within their grasp. As the hour approached, all hope seemed to fade. Then, unexpectedly, at 11:30 P.M., one-half hour before he was to die in the gas chamber, the governor of Louisiana extended a full pardon to the man.
>
> The attorneys were overjoyed as they brought the news to their client. As they told him of his freedom

something happened that brought the state of Louisiana to a stand still. He refused the pardon. At precisely 12:00 midnight, they strapped the man to the chair and within a few moments he was dead. The entire state was in shock. The man had a full pardon, yet he chose to die anyway.

A fierce legal battle soon erupted over the issue: Was the man pardoned because the governor offered the pardon, or was he pardoned when he accepted the pardon? The highest court in the state of Louisiana was the arena for the debate. Ultimately it was decided that the pardon cannot go into effect until it is accepted.

So it is with us. God offers us eternal life, a pardon from sin, yet too often we reject the pardon. God offers the pardon, but we need to accept it.[2]

We have been pardoned. Not only were we set free from the prison of sin, we were also given a new beginning, a fresh start. We were born again to live a new life for Christ. Many people accept the pardon that Jesus offers for the forgiveness of sin but reject the fresh start. Why not take advantage of both offers!

Our Identification with Christ

Another way the Bible describes our renewal at salvation is with concepts related to Christ's death and resurrection. Faith not only unites the believer with Christ, but also unites him with the death and resurrection of Christ. The apostle Paul said, "Don't you know that all of us who were baptized into Christ Jesus were baptized into his death? We were therefore buried with him through baptism into death in order that, just as Christ was raised from the dead . . . we too may live a new life" (Romans 6:3,4).

Paul also wrote, "[God] made us alive with Christ even when we were dead in transgressions" (Ephesians 2:5).

Galatians 2:20 says, "I have been crucified with Christ and I no longer live, but Christ lives in me. The life I live in the body, I live by faith in the Son of God, who loved me and gave himself for me." Paul was saying, "I died, but I live. I'm obviously a new and different person" (see also Colossians 3:1-3). In other words, we as Christians have a new identity, and it comes from who we are in Christ—not who we were in Adam. The apostle Paul identified every believer with Christ:

- In His death (Romans 6:3,6; Galatians 2:20; Colossians 3:1-3)

- In His burial (Romans 6:4)

- In His resurrection (Romans 6:5,8)

- In His ascension (Ephesians 2:6)

- In His life (Romans 6:10,11)

- In His power (Ephesians 1:18-20)

- In His inheritance (Romans 8:16,17; Ephesians 1:11,12)

A New Man

What does it mean to be a "new man"? Does it mean that every aspect of the believer becomes new? This may seem confusing because we still have the same physical appearance, and we still have many of the same thoughts, feelings, and experiences. Because so much appears to be the same when we become Christians, some people say that our newness refers only to our position in Christ. They say that our newness relates only to our being declared righteous (justified), and there is no real change in us until we are finally glorified. However, that would be like teaching we are forgiven, but there is no new life (justification without regeneration). We *have* to believe that our new identity is in the life of Christ and commit ourselves to grow accordingly. A primary work of the Holy Spirit is to bear witness with our spirit that we are children of God (Romans 8:16).

Despite the fact that we live according to the old self at times, we are, in reality, new persons—new in relationship to God and new in ourselves. The change that takes place in us when we come to Christ involves two dimensions. First, we have a new master. As mortals, we have no choice but to live under a spiritual power—either our heavenly Father's, or the god of this world's. But at salvation we experience a change in the power that dominates life. Second, there is an actual change in the nature of the believer so that the deepest desires of his or her heart are now oriented toward God instead of toward self and sin. All of these changes amount to a new identity for the person in Christ.

A New Master

At salvation, when you became identified with Christ in His death and resurrection, you became a new person and part of the new humanity. In this change you came under a new power that has dominion over your life. Nowhere is this expressed more clearly than in Romans 6:5-7:

> If we have been united with him . . . in his death, we will certainly also be united with him in his resurrection. For we know that our old self was crucified with him so that the body of sin might be done away with, that we should no longer be slaves to sin—because anyone who has died has been freed from sin.

In our minds we like to picture two knights: One knight is light. He wears silver armor and sits on a sparkling horse. The armor is polished to a high shine so bright that you can see your reflection in it. That's the new you in Christ. Across from this brave, pure knight is an evil, dark knight. He is sick and twisted—everything about this knight is revolting. He is proud, rebellious, and filled with bitterness. He's experienced every evil imaginable and brags about it. That's the old you before you came to Christ. The two will be locked in combat as long as you live, and the one you let your mind side with will win—*right?*

Wrong! The scene is all wrong. The evil, dark knight *died* when you received Christ. Only his old fleshly habits and fears remain. Carefully reread Romans 6:5-7. Notice that if something is crucified it's dead! The phrase *old self* in this passage is literally "old man." The "old man" in relation to the believer has been crucified in Christ, and the believer has put on the "new man" (Colossians 3:10).

Check It Out!

It is not what we do that determines who we are, it is who we are that determines what we do.

We need to understand that this is a reality that has already taken place. Paul says in Romans 6:6 that "our old self *was* crucified." Some of us try to put the old man to death, and we can't do it. Why? Because he is already dead! We cannot do for ourselves what Christ has already done for us. Because many Christians are not living the abundant life, they incorrectly reason, "What has to happen in order for me to experience the life of the new man?" The only thing that has to happen already happened nearly 2,000 years ago—and the only way you can enter into that experience is by faith.

It is not *what* we do that determines who we are, it is *who* we are that determines what we do. We don't serve God with the hope that someday He will accept us. We already are accepted into God's family; that is why we serve Him.

Too many young Christians are trying to prove that the Bible is true by the way they live. It will never work. We believe what God says is true and live accordingly by faith, and then it works out in our lives. If we try to make it true by our experience, we will never get there. Paul points out the futility of such thinking in Galatians 3:2: "I would like to learn just one thing from you: Did you receive the Spirit by observing the law, or by believing what you heard? Are you so foolish? After beginning with the Spirit, are you now trying to attain your goal by human effort?"

We are saved by faith, and we walk or live by faith. We have been sanctified by faith, and we are being sanctified by faith. We are neither saved nor sanctified by how we behave, but by how we believe.

Freedom from Sin and Death

When we become new creations in Christ, there is a change of dominion over our lives. Both the old and new spheres of life—or the old man and new man—are determined by events and the powers associated with them. The old man is determined by the sin of Adam and is, therefore, dominated by the power of sin. The new man is determined by the righteous obedience of Christ and is ruled by the power of the new resurrection life of Christ. Dying to the old sphere of existence means dying to the powers that dominated it and coming into a new life under a new power.

The change of power over our lives as believers is described by the apostle Paul in Romans 6:6,7. Our old self—that is, our unregenerate self as individuals existing in the old natural sphere of sinfulness—was crucified so that the "body of sin might be done away with, that we should no longer be slaves to sin." Before we became new creations in Christ, we were slaves to sin (Romans 6:16,17; 7:23,25). We had no choice because we were born physically alive but spiritually dead. The Bible says that "sin reigned in death" (Romans 5:21) and, thus, death reigned over us (5:14,17). Living in the sphere of the old man included slavery to the law (see Romans 7:1-6; Galatians 4:9). This is not in the sense that the law is sin, but that living in the sphere of the old man and sin we were under the curse of the law (Galatians 3:13). But our slavery to the sins we were involved in has come to an end through our death and resurrection in Christ.

Free to Live Abundantly

The way to the goal of freedom from sin is through death. When a person dies, sin loses its mastery over that person. Because the believer has died *with Christ* (participated with Him in His death to sin), he is free from the mastery of sin and lives a new life of freedom. Paul said:

> Just as you used to offer the parts of your body in slavery to impurity and to ever-increasing wickedness, so now offer them in slavery to righteousness leading to holiness. When you were slaves to sin, you were free from the control of

> righteousness. . . . But now that you have been set
> free from sin and have become slaves to God, the
> benefit you reap leads to holiness, and the result is
> eternal life (Romans 6:19,20,22).

Because of our union with Christ in His death and resurrection, we too live spiritually and eternally in newness of life—a life over which death (including physical death) has no power. This truth is made clear by Paul in Romans 6:8,9: "Now if we died with Christ, we believe that we will also live with him. For we know that since Christ was raised from the dead, he cannot die again; death no longer has mastery over him." Paul is so confident of this truth that he writes, "For to me, to live is Christ and to die is gain" (Philippians 1:21). Put anything else in the formula, and it doesn't work. For me to live is straight A's, then to die would be loss. Or, for me to live is my girlfriend/boyfriend, and again to die would be loss (well, we're assuming you have a nice girlfriend/boyfriend).

Because death no longer has mastery over you, all that will happen when you die physically is you'll receive a resurrected body and be ushered into the presence of God. The person who is free from the fear of death is really free to live the abundant life in Christ "because through Christ Jesus the law of the Spirit of life set [him] free from the law of sin and death" (Romans 8:2).

Just as the proclamation of emancipation brought freedom to the slaves in America, so too has the gospel brought freedom to us. The god of this world is to us as many plantation owners were to their slaves. Both wanted to be served, and neither wanted people to know of their freedom.

The god of this world will try to keep you from the truth that sets you free. Would you like a little story to illustrate this point? Say yes! Good.

Once upon a time there was a lion who had been lost just after his birth. Fortunately for him, he was rescued and subsequently raised by a mother sheep. She raised him just the way she raised her other sheep children. She taught him to eat grass and, although his teeth grew large and his jaw muscles bulged, he continued to eat grass. She also taught him to baa-baa like a sheep. Although his lungs grew big and strong, he still would baa-baa. And of course she taught him to walk. And although he tiptoed around like a little dainty sheep, he still seemed to have the urge to do so much more.

One day, after he had grown into a strong and mature lion, he happened upon a group of lions. He noticed how they roared loudly and convincingly and how they galloped, leaped, and ran the way their powerful legs were meant to do. They shared a piece of meat with him and it tasted uniquely sweet. He loved the way his massive teeth cut the meat into bite size pieces and his jaws could even crush bone. And then it hit him. "I'm a lion!" he said and with that he ran back and ate all the sheep....*No!* I told you this wasn't a sad story. With that he ran and joined the lions.[3]

The world, the flesh, and the devil want you to believe you're still a product of your sinful past. But your new relationship with Jesus has opened your eyes to the real person you are in Christ.

But Why Do I Still Sin?

If we are now free in Christ and we are new creatures, then why do we still sin every now and then? Let's take a look at why we still serve the old slaveries of sin and death sometimes.

Since we were born physically alive but spiritually dead, we had neither the presence of God in our lives nor the knowledge of His ways. So, during those formative years of our lives, we learned how to live independently of God as a "natural" person. When we came to Christ, we were born again and each of us became a brand-new creation in Him. Unfortunately, everything that was previously programmed into our minds was still there. Nobody pushed the delete or clear button as is done when erasing stuff on a computer. That's why Romans 12:2 says, "Do not conform any longer to the pattern of this world, but be transformed by the renewing of your mind." Even as Christians we can still choose to conform to this world by reading inappropriate magazines, thinking ungodly thoughts, going to R-rated movies, and having the wrong friends.

The apostle Paul had been trained under the law, a "Hebrew of Hebrews; in regard to the law, a Pharisee" (Philippians 3:5). After conversion his "old man" (self) was dead, and he wrote, "I consider everything a loss compared to the surpassing greatness of knowing Christ Jesus my Lord" (Philippians 3:8). We have a new master who has come to set the captives free from sin and death. God has "rescued us from the dominion of darkness and brought us into the kingdom of the Son he loves" (Colossians 1:13).

Under the dominion of God and His Son, the grace and righteousness of God dominates our lives. In fact, we have become slaves to righteousness, which leads to holiness. This truth shows that we have not simply exchanged one master for another—our new servitude to God leads to a fullness of life that can be spoken of as "our reigning in life."

When speaking of our being under another master, keep in mind that we are not talking about doing away with our own responsibilities or power to choose. Yes, there is a certain freedom on the part of the human being to present himself or herself to the master (Romans 6:13,19; 12:1). Nevertheless, who a person chooses to serve will be the dominant influence in the actions and choices under which he or she lives.

A New Person with New Desires

Identifying with Christ in His death and resurrection involves more than an external change of master. It also involves a *transformation within* ourselves. Our very being is changed at its deepest level so that we now have new desires.

The newness of our person or self is seen clearly in the fact that we have been given a new heart. According to Scripture, our heart is who we really are as a person.[4] "As water reflects a face, so a man's heart reflects the man" (Proverbs 27:19).

God knows who we really are because He looks at our hearts. In the Old Testament, Samuel could not understand why God had passed up the older sons of Jesse in favor of David. But God replied, "The LORD does not look at the things man looks at. Man looks at the outward appearance, but the LORD looks at the heart" (1 Samuel 16:7). In the New Testament, Peter encourages godly women to make their beauty the qualities of the "hidden person of the heart" (1 Peter 3:4 NASB).

What needs to be changed is the heart. The heart not only reflects who we are, it also directs our lives. We live according to the condition of our hearts. That's why

Proverbs 4:23 tells us, "Above all else, guard your heart, for it is the wellspring of life."

In Hebrew, the last part of Proverbs 4:23 literally means "for out of it are the issues of life." The heart is not only the fountain of life, it also controls the course of life. The direction that our lives take is determined by the heart. This is seen in Ecclesiastes 10:2: "A wise man's heart *directs* him toward the right, but the foolish man's heart *directs* him toward the left" (NASB, emphasis added).

Jesus taught that what we do comes from the heart: "Out of the overflow of the heart the mouth speaks." This is beautifully illustrated in this story:

> A successful beauty company asked people in a large city to send brief letters and pictures about the most beautiful woman they knew. Within a few weeks thousands of letters were delivered to the company.
>
> One letter in particular caught the attention of the employees, and soon it was handed to the company president. The letter was written by a young boy who was obviously from a broken home and living in a run-down neighborhood. With spelling corrected, an excerpt from his letter reads: "A beautiful woman lives down the street from me. I visit her every day. She makes me feel like the most important kid in the world. We play checkers and she listens to my problems. She understands me and when I leave she always yells out the door that she's proud of me."
>
> The boy ended his letter saying, "This picture shows you that she is the most beautiful woman. I hope I have a wife as pretty as her."
>
> Intrigued by the letter, the president asked to see this woman's picture. The secretary handed him the photograph of a smiling, toothless woman, well advanced in years, sitting in a wheelchair. Sparse gray hair was pulled

back in a bun and wrinkles that formed deep furrows on her face were somehow diminished by the twinkle in her eyes.

"We can't use this woman," explained the president, smiling. "She would show the world that our products aren't necessary to be beautiful."⁵

Our whole life stems from our heart. Our thoughts, motives, words, feelings, attitudes, and actions all originate in the heart. As one person said, the heart is the "mission control center of human life."⁶ The believer in Christ, through death and resurrection with Him, has received a new heart and a new command center of life. This is necessary because it is the nature of the human heart to be controlled by an outside master. This is due to the fact that we are not the source of our lives. We do not have the fountain of life in us. The heart and soul of man was never designed by God to function as master. We are dependent creatures and must look outside of ourselves—to Christ—for life.

What the heart takes in also becomes its master, stamping the heart with its character. That's why it's so important to be careful what we let in. Jesus told His disciples to store up treasures that could not be destroyed: "Where your treasure is, there your heart will be also" (Matthew 6:21).

The change of masters from the dominion of sin to the rule of God and His Son, which happened when we became Christians, has effected a real change in us and our lives.

Desiring Change

The Old Testament revealed that the "heart is deceitful above all things and beyond cure" (Jeremiah 17:9). While the heart of the Christian still carries remnants of the old, the deepest desire of the believer has been changed. This truth is seen in Paul's words to the Galatians: "Because you are sons, God sent the Spirit of his Son

into our hearts, the Spirit who calls out, 'Abba, Father'"
(4:6). The cry, "Abba, Father!" is typical of a son speaking intimately with his father and represents the
believer's most basic relationship with God. This cry is
determined by the presence of the Spirit, who brings
Christ the Son into the center of our personality to live
within our hearts.

The primary desire of the human heart is love. And it
is our love that finally determines our identity. The presence of sin in the life of the believer indicates that remnants of the old, disordered love of self remains. But those
remnants now stand at the outside edges of the real core
of the person, who is God-oriented and bent toward righteousness. The identity of the believer is someone who
loves God rather than sin.

The true Christian, in the depth of his heart, has a nature
that is turned toward God. Although he can still sin, this sin
is related to a more surface level of his being (which can still
act contrary to the real person of the heart). But these surface actions are temporary and do not change the nature of
the heart and, thus, the person's identity. In fact, this very
issue may be the surest way to determine whether or not a
person is a Christian. If someone does something that is
contrary to the nature of God and feels no remorse or conviction, then we could legitimately question his salvation.
On the other hand, we have talked to hundreds of young
people who are questioning their own salvation because
they are struggling in their Christian walks. In almost every
case, after hearing these young people's testimonies, we do
what we can to *assure* them of their salvation. After all, what
they are struggling with wouldn't even bother them if they
weren't already Christians.

Our Hearts Affect Our Actions

The true nature of a person does not always express itself fully in his or her life, but the basic identity of that person is still there. And in the case of the believer, it is positive toward God. This is clearly evident in Paul's description of a believer in Romans 7:14-25:

> We know that the law is spiritual; but I am unspiritual, sold as a slave to sin. I do not understand what I do. For what I want to do I do not do, but what I hate I do. And if I do what I do not want to do, I agree that the law is good. As it is, it is no longer I myself who do it, but it is sin living in me. I know that nothing good lives in me, that is, in my flesh. For I have the desire to do what is good, but I cannot carry it out. For what I do is not the good I want to do; no, the evil I do not want to do—this I keep on doing.
>
> Now if I do what I do not want to do, it is no longer I who do it, but it is sin living in me that does it. So I find this law at work: When I want to do good, evil is right there with me. For in my inner being I delight in God's law; but I see another law at work in the members of my body, waging war against the law of my mind and making me a prisoner of the law of sin at work within my members. What a wretched man I am! Who will rescue me from this body of death? Thanks be to God—through Jesus Christ our Lord! So then, I myself in my mind am a slave to God's law, but in the...[flesh] a slave to the law of sin (Romans 7:14-25).

This passage seems to be describing someone who has experienced the renewing grace of God. But it also shows this person in relation to the law of God apart from the enabling work of the Spirit of God.

We can be certain this person is not an unbeliever because of his likes and dislikes. A true believer desires to do what is good. Does the natural man delight in God's law? When we as Christians make public stands for the sake of justice and righteousness according to the Word of God, do unbelievers around us "agree that the law is good"?

Those descriptions of the personal character of Paul clearly show him to be someone with a positive nature.

Romans 7 shows that the man's heart, that is his mind, his will, and emotions were directed toward God. . . . It also shows that the law is powerless to help him.

The Romans 7:14-25 passage presents the real person of the believer as having positive desires toward God and His ways. Though at times the believer commits wrongs both in thought and act, sin and righteousness do not in any way characterize the believer in the same way. The believer is capable of experiencing a double life, serving two masters, as indicated by Paul's words: "I myself in my mind am a slave to God's law, but in the…[flesh] a slave to the law of sin" (verse 25).[7] This statement, along with the entire passage, confirms that the real person of the believer willingly serves God.

Every believer's nature has positive desires toward God; this is true of the most defeated Christian. He may still have remnants of his old desires, but they are not dominant anymore. His heart has been changed so that his deepest desire is now toward God and His way. The new prevailing desire is a love for God and a love for that which is God— that is, His Son, His people, and His righteous ways.

A Vital Understanding

Through death and resurrection with Christ, the real "inner person of the heart" has been born again. A new seed of life has been planted in the heart whose natural tendency, as is the case in all seeds, is to grow. It is absolutely vital that the believer understand this reality as a foundation for growth. Otherwise, maturity in the Christian life and victory over sin is impossible.

Not understanding who we are in Christ can truly hinder our walk with God. The following testimony by one of our former students illustrates this truth. He was one of the most gifted, personable, and intelligent students that we have had the privilege of teaching. He attended one of Neil's seminars and later wrote him this letter:

> I've always figured I was a rotten, no-good, dirty, stinking sinner saved by grace yet failing God miserably every day. And all I could look forward to was a lifetime of apologizing every night for not being the man I know He wants me to be, "But I'll try harder tomorrow, Lord." As a first-born, trying so hard to earn the approval of highly expectant parents, I've related to God in the same way. He just couldn't possibly love me as much as

He does other, "better" believers. Oh sure, I'm saved by grace through faith, but really I'm just hanging on until He gets tired of putting up with me here and brings me home to finally stop the failure in progress. Whew, what a treadmill!

When you said, "You're not a sinner, you're a saint" in reference to our new identity in Christ, you totally blew me away! Isn't that strange that a guy could go clear through a good Christian school and never latch onto the truth that he is, indeed, a new creation in Christ?! I'm convinced that old tapes, laid down in early childhood, can truly hinder our progress in understanding who we are in Christ.

Thank you for your clear teaching in this area. It has been so helpful and liberating to me. I'm beginning to grow out of my old negative thoughts about myself and God. I don't constantly picture Him as disappointed in me any more. I have been so deeply touched by what I've learned that I'm taking some people through a study of Ephesians so we can see who we are *in Christ* and what we have as believers *in Christ*.

Sold Out

Read

John 15:1-15

Reflect

Considering the lesson from the ornamental orange tree and the navel orange tree, are we identified by the root stock or by what grows above the graft line? (Check out Matthew 7:20; 2 Corinthians 5:16,17; and John 15:1-5.)

When you were grafted into the new vine, you were sanctified (set apart) as a child of God. And you will continue to be sanctified as He prunes you so that you can bear more fruit. What evidence of pruning and growth do you see in your life?

"It is not what we do that determines who we are; it is who we are that determines what we do." What freedom does that truth offer?

Explain why growth and victory in the Christian life is impossible unless you understand who you are in Christ. When did you first realize the truth that you're not a sinner but a saint?

Respond

Dear heavenly Father, thank You for grafting me into Your family. I know that I am able to bear fruit because I am connected to You. I also know that without You I can't even do one thing. I want to abide in Christ and bear lots of fruit to show everyone around me how much I really love You. I want to give You total control of my life and have only one master, Jesus, in my life. Help me, Lord, to be quick to realize when I sin and do something Jesus wouldn't do. I want to live a life that shows others I'm alive in Christ and dead to sin. Help me crucify all my old sinful habits and make new holy habits that please You. In Jesus' name I pray, amen.

*I urge you
to live a life worthy
of the calling
you have received.*
—EPHESIANS 4:1

He is no fool who
gives what he cannot keep
to gain what he cannot lose.[1]

—*Jim Elliot*

6

Making the New You Real

The Christian life is full of what appear to be contradictions. The path to glorification is death (John 12:23-25), and the path to exaltation is humiliation (Philippians 2:8,9). The first shall be last (Luke 13:30), and the one who wishes to save his life must lose it. Understanding the truth of this last statement is another key for Christian growth and living. Check out Jesus' words to His disciples in Matthew 16:24-26:

> If anyone would come after me, he must deny
> himself and take up his cross and follow me. For

whoever wants to save his life will lose it, but whoever loses his life for me will find it. What good will it be for a man if he gains the whole world, yet forfeits his soul? Or what can a man give in exchange for his soul?

There's a story told of a famous man called Principal Cairns, who was so humble that he would never even enter a room first. He would always stand aside and say to his companion, "You first. I'll follow."

On one occasion this man was among the honored guests at some public event. As he stepped onto the platform, the audience saw Cairns and erupted in applause. Upon hearing their applause, he stopped in his tracks. He motioned for the man behind him to go first, assuming that the clapping and cheering was for that man. He then stood back and joined the applause. He never dreamed the applause could be for him.

Of course, such sincere humility impressed people and brought even greater honor to Principal Cairns. That's similar to what Jesus meant when He said, "The proud will be humbled, but the humble will be honored" (Luke 14:11). When you act like you think you're big and important, it can be embarrassing to find out that you're not as big or not as important as you thought. But when you're humble enough to let other people get the applause and attention, you may be surprised at how much people appreciate you and honor you.[2]

If what the Lord is saying is not understood and personally put into practice, then fulfilling the great commission (going into all the world and making disciples) and the great commandment (loving God and your neighbor as yourself) will not be possible.

The occasion of Jesus' words in Matthew 16 was immediately after Peter's great confession that Jesus was the Christ, the Son of the living God (Matthew 16:16). Jesus assured Peter that flesh and blood had not revealed that truth to him, but rather His Father in heaven.

Then Jesus foretold His death and resurrection in Jerusalem. Peter couldn't believe what he was hearing and rebuked Jesus: "'Never, Lord!' he said, 'This shall never happen to you!'" (Matthew 16:22). Jesus responded by saying, "Get behind me, Satan! You are a stumbling block to me; you do not have in mind the things of God, but the things of men" (verse 23). Peter, the one who confessed Jesus as the Messiah, the Son of the living God, suddenly finds himself the mouthpiece of Satan, the deceiver.

This rebuke seems really tough, yet Christ's crediting of Satan as the source describes exactly and appropriately the *character* of the advice given by Peter: Save yourself at any rate, sacrifice duty to self-interest and the cause of Christ to personal convenience. This advice is truly satanic for the whole aim of Satan is to get self-interest recognized as the chief end of man. Satan is called the "ruler of this world" because self-interest runs it. He is called the "accuser of the brethren" because he does not believe that even the sons of God have any higher motive:

> Does Job or even Jesus serve God for nothing? Self-sacrifice, suffering for righteousness' sake, commitment to truth even unto death: it is pure romance and youthful sentimentalism or at best, hypocritical. There is no such thing as a surrender of the lower life for the higher life; all men are selfish at heart and have their price. Some may hold out longer than others, but in the end every man will prefer his own thing to the things of God.

Such is Satan's creed. And man unwittingly serves Satan, when he's deceived into thinking that he is serving himself. Jesus counters by sharing the way of the cross: "If anyone would come after me, he must deny himself and take up his cross and follow me" (Matthew 16:24). Such a statement seems crazy—as though the Lord is asking for everything and promising very little. Nothing could be further from the truth because he who wants to save his life will eventually lose it. Anyone who looks for his or her identity, fulfillment, or purpose for living in the natural world will lose everything. You cannot take your earthly gain with you. Whatever treasures you are able to store up on planet Earth will remain here after you die physically.

If you crucify the flesh and find your life in Christ, you will have the benefit of knowing Him now and for all eternity. If you shoot for this world you will miss the next, but if you shoot for the next world you will actually receive the benefits of living in Christ right now (as well as in eternity). Paul says, "Discipline yourself for the purpose of godliness; for bodily discipline is only of little profit, but godliness is profitable for all things, since it holds promise for the present life and also for the life to come" (1 Timothy 4:7,8 NASB). He's not saying that we shouldn't take care of ourselves physically. He is saying that taking care of the body has little value compared to disciplining ourselves spiritually.

Denying ourselves is the only way to put Christ back into the center of our lives. Some young people perceive lordship as a bad deal, but it's not. Making Jesus the Lord of our lives is our only hope for now and for eternity. If we make Him the Lord of our lives, then He is the Lord of our past, present, and future. He is also the Lord of all our problems, and we can "cast all [our] anxiety on him because he cares for [us]" (1 Peter 5:7). God is not out to get us; He is out to redeem us and restore us to the state in which Adam was originally created.

For some unknown reason, it seems that the great ambition of mankind is to be happy as animals instead of being blessed as children of God. But the reward of being a child of God is so much greater. When you deny yourself, identify with Christ, and follow Him daily, you sacrifice the pleasure of things, but you gain the pleasure of life. You sacrifice the temporal to gain the eternal. Some sacrifice! It would be foolish to sacrifice your soul to gain in this world that which you cannot take with you.

So what do we who are liberated slaves do to live like free people? We don't begin by denying the reality of sin. We start by growing through the realization of who we are in Christ. The Bible teaches that progressive sanctification is making our position in Christ and the newness of our person through regeneration increasingly real in daily life. It involves turning from the attitude and practice of sin, with all of their negative effects in life, to that of the attitude and practice of righteousness with all of their positive effects.

Sin's Presence in the Believer's Life

John makes it clear in 1 John 1:7-10 that believers are still involved with sin:

> If we walk in the light, as he is in the light, we have fellowship with one another, and the blood of Jesus, his Son, purifies us from all sin. If we claim to be without sin, we deceive ourselves and the truth is not in us. If we confess our sins, he is faithful and just and will forgive us our sins and purify us from all unrighteousness. If we claim we have not sinned, we make him out to be a liar and his word has no place in our lives.

We are continually being cleansed from sin as we walk in the light. Walking in the light doesn't mean sinless perfection because, as we just read, we deceive ourselves if we say we have no sin.

It is important to understand that "having sin" and "being sin" are two different things. Walking in the light is living in agreement with our heavenly Father. It is essentially the same as *confessing*, which means "to agree with God." This verse doesn't tell us to ask God for forgiveness because we are already forgiven, but we do need to live honestly and openly before God. If it's necessary for believers to continually be cleansed from sin, then they must somehow have sin.

That sin is present in the new person is also affirmed in Paul's description of a continual battle going on in the believer: "I say, walk by the Spirit, and you will not carry out the desire of the flesh. For the flesh sets its desire against the Spirit, and the Spirit against the flesh; for these are in opposition to one another" (Galatians 5:16,17 NASB). The battlefield of this war is the life of every believer. This combat with sin is what Paul talks about when he tells us to be continually "putting to death the deeds of the body" (Romans 8:13 NASB).

To help us grow away from sin, our heavenly Father disciplines us as His children so that we may share in His holiness and reap a harvest of righteousness and peace (Hebrews 12:5-11). Frequently we are told to stop various sins (see, for example, Ephesians 4:25-32; Colossians 3:5-9) and pursue holiness and purity (2 Corinthians 7:1). Even the apostle Paul, as great as he was, acknowledged that he was still pressing on toward the goal of knowing Christ more completely and that he had not already been made perfect (Philippians 3:12).

All of these Bible passages show that even though we are new persons in Christ, with new dominant desires toward God and His holiness, we still sin. Sin no longer reigns over us, but it still dwells within us. Growth in holiness means increasingly putting off the sinful desires and their actions by deepening our daily realization of our newness and the truth that we really are in Christ.

You've Already Been Changed

We saw in Romans 6:6 that our old self was crucified with Christ when we united with Him by faith. This was a decisive and definite act in the believer's past. Growth in holiness takes place when we claim the reality of these past events and act on them. That is Paul's point in Ephesians 4:22-24 when he says,

> You were taught, with regard to your former way of life, to put off your old self, which is being corrupted by its deceitful desires; to be made new in the attitude of your minds; and to put on the new self, created to be like God in true righteousness and holiness.

We need to renew our minds to the truth that a change *has* taken place in us and then live accordingly by faith, with the confidence that it will work out in our experience. We are no longer slaves to sin, but we must assume our responsibility to no longer think and act like slaves.

Putting on Christ

Just as putting on the new man is both a past act and a present challenge, so also is the putting on of Christ a past and present matter. Paul says in Galatians 3:27, "All of you who were baptized into Christ have clothed yourselves with Christ." (The Greek word translated "clothed your-selves" is the same word translated "put on" in relation to the new self [man] in Ephesians 4:24 and Colossians 3:10, and can be translated "put on Christ.")

To clothe oneself with, or to put on a person, "means to take on the characteristics, virtues, and/or intentions of the one referred to, and so to become like that person."[3] Paul is saying that when we came to Christ, we were joined to Him—we were made alive in Him. We became a partaker of the divine nature and began the process of becoming like Him (2 Peter 1:4). God didn't simply give us the power to imitate Him; He actually reconciled us to Himself so that our souls are in union with His! F.F. Bruce says, "Be in ordinary practice what God's grace has made you."[4] We are to assume responsibility for becoming what we already are in Christ by the grace of God.

Spiritual Metamorphosis

God has given us many pictures in nature to show us the wonderful transformation that salvation brings. Con-sider the plight of the caterpillar. It crawls on the surface of the earth with tiny suction cup-like legs. Four times during its life, the caterpillar grows out of its own skin, which is a sign of what is to come. This fuzzy little worm also happens to eat what it has shed because it is rich in protein. What it was plays a part in what it will be.

One day, as though led by instinct, it climbs as high as it can by its own strength—usually on the limb of a tree or on a small branch. There it creates a little button that forms an attachment for the cocoon that it spins around itself as it hangs upside down. The caterpillar then ceases to exist, and a miraculous transformation takes place. In the caterpillar's place is a butterfly that eventually fights its way out and learns to fly. The caterpillar "crucified" itself in order to be "resurrected" a butterfly. It gave up the security of its own limited resources and earthbound existence in order to fly. Though a caterpillar would appear to be much stronger than a butterfly, it cannot escape the law of gravity. The butterfly is the more fragile creature, but it can gracefully soar in freedom. The caterpillar gave up all that it was in order to become all that the Creator designed it to become. It gave up its short stubby legs for beautiful wings.

Now, imagine what would happen to the growth of the new butterfly if it chose to believe that it was still a caterpillar. It would come nowhere near to reaching its potential. Likewise, when we who are new in Christ perceive that we are still the old self, we won't experience the fullness of the Christian life as God intended.

By the way, just as the caterpillar cannot take credit for becoming a butterfly, we cannot take credit for the work of Christ which is given to us by the grace of God. We can only receive Christ's work by faith, and we must continuously choose to believe who we already are in Christ in order to become what we were created to be. If we think and act like caterpillars, the Lord will receive no glory for what He did on our behalf.

So that you might have a better understanding of who you are in Christ, we've included this following list of Scriptures from Neil and Dave's book *Stomping Out the Darkness*:[5]

WHO AM I?

Matthew 5:13:   I am the salt of the earth.

Matthew 5:14:   I am the light of the world.

John 1:12:	I am a child of God (part of His family —see Romans 8:16).
John 15:1,5:	I am part of the *true* vine, a channel (branch) of His (Christ's) life.
John 15:15:	I am Christ's friend.
John 15:16:	I am chosen and appointed by Christ to bear *His* fruit.
Romans 6:18:	I am a slave of righteousness.
Romans 6:22:	I am enslaved to God.
Romans 8:14,15:	I am a son of God (God is spiritually my Father—see Galatians 3:26 and 4:6).
Romans 8:17:	I am a joint-heir with Christ, sharing His inheritance with Him.
1 Corinthians 3:16; 6:19:	I am a temple (home) of God. His Spirit (His life) dwells in me.
1 Corinthians 6:17:	I am joined (united) to the Lord and am one spirit with Him.
1 Corinthians 12:27:	I am a member (part) of Christ's body (see Ephesians 5:30).
2 Corinthians 5:17:	I am a new creation (new person).
2 Corinthians 5:18,19:	I am reconciled to God and am a minister of reconciliation.
Galatians 3:26,28:	I am a son of God and one in Christ.
Galatians 4:6,7:	I am an heir of God since I am a son of God.
Ephesians 1:1:	I am a saint (see 1 Corinthians 1:2; Philippians 1:1; and Colossians 1:2).

Ephesians 2:10:	I am God's workmanship (handiwork) created (born anew) in Christ to do His work that He planned beforehand that I should do.
Ephesians 2:19:	I am a fellow citizen with the rest of God's people in His family.
Ephesians 3:1; 4:1:	I am a prisoner of Christ.
Ephesians 4:24:	I am righteous and holy.
Philippians 3:20:	I am a citizen of heaven and seated in heaven right now (see Ephesians 2:6).
Colossians 3:3:	I am hidden with Christ in God.
Colossians 3:4:	I am an expression of the life of Christ because He is my life.
Colossians 3:12:	I am chosen of God, holy, and dearly loved.
1 Thessalonians 1:4:	I am chosen and dearly loved by God.
1 Thessalonians 5:5:	I am a son of light and not of darkness.
Hebrews 3:1:	I am a holy brother, partaker of a heavenly calling.
Hebrews 3:14:	I am a partaker of Christ. I share in His life.
1 Peter 2:5:	I am one of God's living stones and am being built up (in Christ) as a spiritual house.
1 Peter 2:9,10:	I am a chosen race, a royal priesthood, a holy nation, a people for God's own possession to proclaim the excellencies of Him.

1 Peter 2:11:	I am an alien and stranger to this world I temporarily live in.
1 Peter 5:8:	I am an enemy of the devil.
1 John 3:1,2:	I am now a child of God. I will resemble Christ when He returns.
1 John 5:18:	I am born of God, and the evil one (the devil) cannot touch me.

I am not the great "I AM" (Exodus 3:14; John 8:24, 28,58), "but by the grace of God I am what I am" (1 Corinthians 15:10).

You're walking down the street, minding your own business, when you hear something. "Psst!" a voice says. You stop and turn. A thin man in dark glasses leans against the side of a building.

"Hey, Slick," the man says, casting furtive glances left and right. "You wanna make the smartest deal of your life?"

You start to turn and walk away, when the man hustles around in front of you and, after a quick glance up and down the sidewalk, opens one side of his coat. There, pinned to the inside of the fabric, is a row of…baseball cards.

"I've got a 1953 Walt Zambrisky card for thirteen cents," the man says.

You shake your head and try to walk around the baseball-card hawker.

"OK, OK," he says, as he backpedals up the sidewalk ahead of you. "I can tell you're a smart customer." He opens the coat again and points to a card. "A Bruno Gunderschmutz rookie card, mint condition, seventy-five cents." He wags his eyebrows as if they were battery operated.

You make a move to pass him again, but he holds up both hands. "OK, OK," he says, "you must want the good stuff." He steals a glance over your shoulder. "My last offer. Mickey Mantle. Rookie card. One thousand smackaroonies."

A thousand dollars? For a baseball card? Actually, yes! Some cards have sold for more than that. Sports cards have become a valuable commodity, an investment.

But what makes a Mickey Mantle rookie card worth a thousand dollars and a Bruno Gunderschmutz rookie card worth only seventy-five cents? After all, they're both made of nothing but cardboard and ink. What's the difference? Just one thing: the image on the card. A Mickey Mantle card bears the image of a New York Yankees slugger who broke Babe Ruth's record for World Series home runs and was later elected to the Baseball Hall of Fame. It's not what the card is made of that makes it valuable; it's the image that appears on the card.[6]

It's sort of the same way because of the new life we have in Christ. We are valuable because of the image that we bear. You may be tall or you may be short. You may be skinny or fat, rich or poor but none of that determines who you really are! It is *who you are in Christ* that counts. The new identity that is ours in Christ made something that was sinful and worthless into something eternal and holy. We need to renew our minds with the truth that a change *has* taken place in us and then live accordingly. What do you see when you look in the mirror: a 1953 Walt Zambrisky worth 13 cents or a child of God who's priceless?

Living Out What You Really Are

The idea of Christian growth being the process of living out what happened at salvation is seen in several calls to live according to what God has already done for and in us. Paul says, "As a prisoner for the Lord, then, I urge you to live a life worthy of the calling you have received" (Ephesians 4:1). Left on our own we would be nothing more than caterpillars with no other purpose in life than to "eat and drink, for tomorrow we die" (1 Corinthians 15:32). But God has called us out of darkness into light.

The point we are trying to make is that in progressive sanctification believers are making true in their experience their new position in Christ and their relationship with God by living out their "calling." Peter says:

> You are a chosen people, a royal priesthood, a holy nation, a people belonging to God, that you may declare the praises of him who called you out of darkness into his wonderful light. Once you were not a people, but now you are the people of God; once you had not received mercy, but now you have received mercy (1 Peter 2:9,10).

"Transformation" refers to a change in which a person's true inner condition is shown outwardly.

Can you imagine the exhilaration of emerging from the darkness of a cocoon into the light? We have seen that same exhilaration on the faces of thousands of young people when they found their freedom in Christ and realized who they were as children of God.

Being a chosen people and a royal priesthood is both a privilege and a responsibility. The following Scriptures encourage us to live a life worthy of our calling: "Conduct yourselves in a manner worthy of the gospel of Christ" (Philippians 1:27); "live a life worthy of the Lord" (Colossians 1:10); and "live lives worthy of God, who calls you into his kingdom and glory" (1 Thessalonians 2:12).

Understanding Transformation

A clear evidence that sanctification is the realization of what we already are as new people is seen in the biblical teaching of transformation. Paul writes, "Now the Lord is the Spirit, and where the Spirit of the Lord is, there is freedom. And we, who with unveiled faces all reflect the Lord's glory, are being transformed into his likeness with ever-increasing glory, which comes from the Lord, who is the Spirit" (2 Corinthians 3:17,18). Elsewhere Paul writes, "Be transformed by the renewing of your mind" (Romans 12:2). We are in the process of transformation. The word "transformation" refers to a change in which a person's true inner condition is shown outwardly. This is illustrated for us in the transfiguration of Jesus (Matthew 17:1-3). The Greek word for *transfiguration* (*metamorphoo*) in relation to Jesus is the same as that used for "transformed" in Romans 12:2 and 2 Corinthians 3:18. That word is the origin of our English word *metamorphose*, which means "to change or be changed in form." In the transfiguration of Jesus, there was not a change in His nature. He was still God and man. Rather, Jesus was letting His true nature of deity shine through or be seen. His divine nature was manifest. When Paul wrote about us being transformed, he was not talking about a change in our real nature, or who we really are. He was referring to becoming outwardly (in our behavior and walk) what we really are in the depth of our beings—new creations in Christ.

Dying and Rising with Christ

The essence of sanctification is dying in order that we might live. This was the pathway of Christ; it is also the pathway to glory for the believer. We find an analogy of this in nature during the winters in the north country. As a child, I (Neil) would walk in the woods and observe the frozen trees, which seemed to be dead. I would snap a small branch in half and wonder if there was any life in it. Then in the spring, new life would burst forth from that which had appeared to be dead. (Christ's resurrection from the dead, which we celebrate every Easter, happened in the spring!)

Another analogy is the new life that comes from every seed that is sown. If you wanted to grow a giant oak tree, what would you do? Plant an oak tree? No, you would plant an acorn. If you could watch the process, you would see that the tiny acorn would die to itself so that out of it a majestic oak tree could grow. The acorn could sit alone and exist for itself, but it would never become what it was intended to be. Similarly, the seeds to become what God intends us to be are sown in every child of God.

Jesus said, "The hour has come for the Son of Man to be glorified. Truly, truly, I say to you, unless a grain of wheat falls into the earth and dies, it remains by itself alone; but if it dies, it bears much fruit" (John 12:23,24). Like the caterpillar who voluntarily attaches itself to the tree in order to hang upside down, we too must realize that the path upward is first downward. In order to be glorified, Jesus had to first die. We too have to die to who we are in Adam and give up all our dreams for self-glorification in the flesh. We must joyfully choose to glorify God in our bodies.

No Pain, No Gain

If we all knew the truth perfectly, none of us would choose to live our lives independently of God. We wouldn't rob ourselves of the blessings of God in order to temporarily satisfy the flesh. We would gladly deny ourselves, pick up our cross daily, and follow Him. Under the inspiration of God, Paul knew that we wouldn't fully understand all that we have in Christ, "who has blessed us in the heavenly realms with every spiritual blessing" (Ephesians 1:3). So after listing all these blessings, Paul says, "I pray also that the eyes of your heart may be enlightened in order that you may know the hope to which he has called you, the riches of his glorious inheritance in the saints" (Ephesians 1:18).

The problem is that "self" will never cast out "self." We have to be led to do that by the Holy Spirit. That's what Paul meant when he said, "We who are alive are always being given over to death for Jesus' sake, so that his life may be revealed in our mortal body" (2 Corinthians 4:11). That is, we often have to struggle to overcome sin even though we have already died to it. Such struggling may appear to be a negative, but it's actually to our benefit. Let's illustrate this. If you saw a butterfly struggling to emerge from its cocoon, would you try to help it? That may seem to be the loving thing to do, but it isn't because that struggle, in part, is what gives the butterfly the strength to fly. You would actually be interfering with the butterfly's potential to fly. The same is true of a baby eagle emerging from its egg.

Whether we walk among the lambs or roar with the lions has much to do with our willingness to overcome the effects of our past. John writes, "He who overcomes will inherit all this, and I will be his God and he will be my son" (Revelation 21:7). No pain, no gain seems to be a principle of life. Therefore, "endure hardship as discipline; God is treating you as sons" (Hebrews 12:7).

If we didn't have a part to play in overcoming the power of sin, then we would all probably wallow in it. Our spiritual growth is connected with our efforts to overcome sin. This is shown in 1 John 2:12-14, where we read that "children" have overcome the penalty of sin, but the "young men" in the faith have overcome the evil one and the power of sin. We must always remember that the god of this world and the prince of power of the air is always roaring around like a hungry lion seeking someone to devour. Learning how to resist the devil and crucify the flesh is a critical part of growing in Christ. The flesh desires to sin, but our new nature in Christ desires to live righteously.

As Christians we are no longer in Adam because we are in Christ. "For as *in Adam* all die, so *in Christ* all will *be made alive*" (1 Corinthians 15:22, emphasis added). Because of our position in Christ we are no longer in the flesh, but since the flesh remains after salvation, we can still choose to walk according to it (that is, we can choose to live as a natural man—the way we did before we were born again). Paul said, "So it is written: 'The first man Adam became a living being'; the last Adam, a life-giving spirit" (1 Corinthians 15:45). We could summarize who we are by looking at the chart on the next page.

Who We Are

In Adam (1 Corinthians 15:22a)		In Christ (1 Corinthians 15:22b)
old man	*by ancestry*	new man
sinful (Ephesians 2:1-3)	*by nature*	partaker of divine nature (2 Peter 1:4)
in the flesh (Romans 8:8)	*by birth*	in the Spirit (Romans 8:9)
walk after the flesh (Galatians 5:19-21)	*by choice*	walk after the Spirit (Galatians 5:22,23) *or* after the flesh

Love's Key Role in Sanctification

If people were fully sanctified children of God, they would be free from their past and be like Christ in character, which is love. Paul says, "The goal of our instruction is love from a pure heart and a good conscience and a sincere faith" (1 Timothy 1:5 NASB). Sanctification is nothing less than God living in us to perfect His nature in us. The fact that God is love makes love the focus of our Christian life. Knowledge of God and union with Him through Christ means a life of love.

Jesus said, "A new command I give you: Love one another. As I have loved you, so you must love one another" (John 13:34). Why would that be a new command? Hasn't it always been a command to love one another?

Actually, apart from Christ, we can't love without reservation. What makes Christ's love so different than our natural love is that His love is not dependent upon its object. God loves us not because we are lovable, but because it is His nature to love us—God is love. That is the only explanation for the assurance that the love of God is unconditional. Human love, in contrast, is selective: "If you love those who love you, what credit is that to you? Even 'sinners' love those who love them" (Luke 6:32). God's love, when it comes into us, enables us to love as He does. "We love because he first loved us" (1 John 4:19). In other words, because we have become a partaker of the divine nature (which is love), we can by the grace of God love the unlovely. When Christ's love is in us, we can reflect His love:

> Carl Coleman was driving to work one morning when he bumped fenders with another motorist. Both cars stopped, and the woman driving the other car got out to survey the damage. She was distraught. It was her fault, she admitted. She dreaded facing her husband. Coleman was sympathetic, but he had to pursue the exchange of license and registration data. She reached into her compartment to retrieve the documents in an envelope. On the first paper to tumble out, written in her husband's distinct hand, were these words: "In case of accident, remember, Honey, it's you I love, not the car."[7]

We can gain a better understanding of the meaning of the word *agape* (love) in the Bible when we realize that it can be used both as a verb and a noun. When used as a noun, it refers to the character of God. For instance, "Love is patient, love is kind" because God is patient and kind. When used as a verb, it describes the sacrificial actions taken by one who seeks to meet the needs of another:

"God so loved the world that he gave his one and only Son . . ." (John 3:16). Jesus' sole purpose was to do the will of God to the point of suffering as He did in Gethesemane. Even then He prayed, "Father . . . not my will, but yours be done" (Luke 22:42).

It could be said that the evidence of John 3:16 being fulfilled in our lives is described in 1 John 3:16-18:

> This is how we know what love is: Jesus Christ laid down his life for us. And we ought to lay down our lives for our brothers. If anyone has material possessions and sees his brother in need but has no pity on him, how can the love of God be in him? Dear children, let us not love with words or tongue but with actions and in truth.

This passage hits on an important point: The capacity to do loving things for other people springs from the nature and character of God within us. We are not first called to do what appears to be loving things for others; we are first called to be like Christ. Loving deeds flow out of our new nature in Christ.

> In 1921, Lewis Lawes became the warden at Sing Sing prison. No prison was tougher than Sing Sing during that time. But when Warden Lawes retired some 20 years later, that prison had become a humanitarian institution. Those who studied the system said credit for the change belonged to Lawes. But when he was asked about the transformation, here's what he said: "I owe it all to my wonderful wife, Catherine, who is buried outside the prison walls."
>
> Catherine Lawes was a young mother with three small children when her husband became the warden. Everybody warned her from the beginning that she should never set foot inside the prison walls, but that didn't stop Catherine! When the first prison baseball game was held,

she went—walking into the gym with her three beautiful kids, and she sat in the stands with the inmates.

Her attitude was: "My husband and I are going to take care of these men, and I believe they will take care of me! I don't have to worry!"

She insisted on getting acquainted with them and their records. She discovered one convicted murderer was blind so she taught him how to read Braille. Years later, he would weep in love for her.

Later Catherine found a deaf-mute in prison. She went to school to learn how to use sign language. Many say [figuratively] that Catherine Lawes was the body of Jesus that came alive again in Sing Sing from 1921–1937.

Then she was tragically killed in a car accident. The next morning Lewis Lawes didn't come to work, so the acting warden took his place. It seemed almost instantly that the prisoners knew something was wrong.

The following day her body was resting in a casket in her home, three-quarters of a mile from the prison. As the acting warden took his early morning walk he was shocked to see a large crowd of the toughest, hardest-looking criminals gathered like a herd of animals at the main gate. He came closer and noticed tears of grief and sadness. He knew how much they loved Catherine. He turned and faced the men, "All right, men you can go. Just be sure and check in tonight!" Then he opened the gates and the parade of criminals walked, without a guard, the three-quarters of a mile to stand in line to pay their final respects to Catherine Lawes. Every one of them checked back in. Every one![8]

Jesus said, "Love the Lord your God with all your heart and with all your soul and with all your mind. This is the first and greatest commandment. And the second is like it: Love your neighbor as yourself. All the Law and the Prophets hang on these two commandments" (Matthew 22:37-40). The last verse implies that the end purpose for the entire prophetic word of God is to fall in love with Him and mankind. The love for God is what ought to drive all our actions. When we love in this way, people are drawn closer to Jesus and hearts are truly changed.

Love Is the Starting Point

Scripture portrays love as the fulfillment of all the commandments and all the righteous acts we show toward other people. If that's the case, then it is crucial for us to focus on the character of God, which is love. When we focus on the source of life we will bear fruit, and *the fruit* of the Spirit is love (Galatians 5:22). Notice that the fruit of the Spirit is *singular*. The other traits listed in Galatians 5:22,23—joy, peace, patience, kindness, goodness, faithfulness, gentleness, and self-control—are characteristics of love. The characteristic of the new person (or the primary characteristic of sanctification) is love.

The contrast between the acts of the old nature (the flesh) and the fruit of the Spirit is the difference between death and life. Deeds done in the flesh without life are dead acts because fruit can only be produced by something that is alive. The flesh can perform certain acts, but the fruit of the Spirit produces character. To be perfected in love is the ultimate goal of being sanctified in Christ.

Once we have fallen in love with God and all that is true and good, we will naturally (or better, supernaturally) fall in love with all others created in the image of God. "Whoever loves God must also love his brother" (1 John 4:21). The love of God compels us to do so.

Sold Out

Matthew 16:24-26; 1 John 1:7-10

Reflect

What is the difference between "having sin" and "being sin"? Why is this significant?

What power do believers have beyond just imitating Christ? How does becoming what we already are in Christ relate to your answer? What does the butterfly teach you about whose power is behind the transformation?

Read through the "Who Am I?" list on page 123–26. Pick three truths that really caught your attention. How do these truths impact how you view yourself? Your actions? Your choices?

How does the call to love one another fit with the work of sanctification God does in His children? What is God's love supposed to do in your life? Why are we first called to be like Christ—and then to love others? Who have you offered unconditional love to lately? Did you grow from that experience? Explain.

Respond

Lord, help me put off the old sinful desires and focus on loving You and those around me. I am so used to putting me first and not even asking You what You want me to do in my life—or even how You want me to do it. I have centered my life around myself rather than around You. I know You have changed me and given me new desires—desires to live for You instead of just for myself. Help me recognize when I'm focusing on the wrong things. Help me focus on You and Your will. Thank You that I'm a new creation in You and that I am alive in You. I know I have the strength to live above the flesh and truly love others because of You. In Jesus' name I pray, amen.

His divine power has given us everything we need for life and godliness through our knowledge of him who called us by his own glory and goodness.

—2 PETER 1:3

It is our heart that is made in the image and likeness of God.[1]

—*Henri Nouwen*

Who's Changing You?

When I (Neil) was growing up on a farm in Minnesota, spring was a busy season of preparing the ground and sowing our seeds. One method of sowing was called *broadcasting*. You simply cast the seeds upon the surface of the earth. Of course, some of the seeds never took root, but most did if it rained right afterward. To spread the seed, we used an end-gate seeder that we mounted on the tailgate of a wagon, which we pulled with a tractor. Broadcasting required at least two people—one to drive the tractor, and one to sit in the wagon and keep the seeder filled.

139

Although the seeder did the actual broadcasting, the power to sow the seed was in the tractor, not the seeder. If the tractor stopped, so did the sowing. But the sowing also stopped if the seeder got clogged or failed to work. Should the latter happen, the tractor was still able to continue supplying all the power and maintain a straight, narrow path toward the end of the row.

We as Christians are like the seeder. We have the privilege of sowing the seed, cultivating it, and watering the plants, but God causes the growth. Notice that we are involved in this process with God: If we don't plant and water nothing grows, but if God doesn't make it grow there will be no harvest. He also supplies the seed that we are called to sow: "He who supplies seed to the sower and bread for food will also supply and increase your store of seed and will enlarge the harvest of your righteousness" (2 Corinthians 9:10). In his first letter to the Corinthians, Paul says:

> I planted the seed, Apollos watered it, but God made it grow. So neither he who plants nor he who waters is anything, but only God, who makes things grow. The man who plants and the man who waters have one purpose, and each will be rewarded according to his own labor. For we are God's fellow workers; you are God's field, God's building (1 Corinthians 3:6-9).

From seed planting to harvest, our sanctification is first and foremost the work of God. He is the one who drives the tractor that supplies all the power, and He furnishes all the seed. He is the *source* of the divine life that is necessary for our growth. We have no resources in ourselves to overcome the power of sin still present in our lives. The Bible makes it very clear that sanctification is the work of God.

At the same time, God's Word also teaches the need for us to assume our responsibility for the continuing process of sanctification. That is only logical since sanctification involves the change of our own self, which includes our thinking, our emotions, and our will.

There is a big difference between what God has done and will do and what our responsibility is. We can try to save ourselves, but it wouldn't do any good. And we shouldn't try to be another person's conscience or make promises that only God can deliver on. We can and should rest in the finished work of Christ, trust in the grace of God to be faithful to His Word, and have confidence that He will continue to be and do all He said He would be and do.

When we fail to recognize the spiritual matters we are responsible for, then we set ourselves up for disappointment.

Our responsibility has been clearly revealed in God's Word. God will not do for us what He has called us to do. In a very real sense He can't. He can only do that which is consistent with His holy nature, and He cannot deviate from His Word. He stays true to His Word. There can be nothing but defeat and disappointment for young Christians who expect God to do for them what He has commanded them to do. They will be just as defeated if they try to do for themselves what God—and only God—can do. For instance, suppose there is a very difficult person in your youth group. He or she continually interrupts the Bible teaching and his lifestyle is far from godly. Soon the people in the group wonder why God doesn't cause him to leave. So they ask, "Why don't You, God? This is Your church, Your youth group; why don't You do something?" Why *doesn't* God do something? Because the Lord has clearly told us that it is *our* responsibility to go to the person first in private. If he or she will not repent, then we are to bring two other witnesses and continue onward in the discipline process outlined for us by Jesus in Matthew 18:15-17. Inner conviction of sin is God's responsibility, but church discipline is our responsibility.

If you become involved in attempting to resolve a spiritual conflict, then the need to know your responsibility in spiritual matters becomes even more critical. Suppose someone has a frightening demonic attack in his room one night. Nearly paralyzed in fear, he cries out to God and asks Him to do something. But God doesn't seem to do anything. So the person asks, "Why not, God? You are all-powerful, and You know what I'm going through right now. Why won't You help me? You can make it stop!" When the attack continues, the person begins to question God's love and concern for him and perhaps even wonders about his own salvation. After all, if he really is a child of God, then wouldn't his loving heavenly Father take care of him?

Of course God would, but whose responsibility is it to submit to God and resist the devil? God has done all He needs to do in order for us to live a victorious Christian life. He has defeated the devil, forgiven our sins, and given us eternal life. He has equipped us with His Holy Spirit, and we are now seated with Christ in the heavenlies. From that position of authority we are to continue the work of Christ on planet Earth. Does the devil have to flee from us if we don't resist him? Probably not! You cannot be passive about taking your place in Christ. You must "put on the full armor of God, so that when the day of evil comes, you may be able to stand your ground, and after you have done everything, to stand" (Ephesians 6:13).

When we fail to recognize the spiritual matters we are responsible for, we set ourselves up for disappointment because we will think that either God isn't at work in our lives or we are spiritual failures because things didn't go the way we expected.

God the Father's Role in Our Sanctification

God is the primary agent of our sanctification because He is the only source of life, righteousness, holiness, love, and truth. In fact, sanctification is the process of God sharing His life with and through us. Paul prayed, "May God himself, the God of peace, sanctify you through and through. May your whole spirit, soul and body be kept blameless at the coming of our Lord Jesus Christ. The one who calls you is faithful and he will do it" (1 Thessalonians 5:23,24). The truth that God is the primary agent of sanctification is also shown in 2 Peter 1:3-9, which goes into specific detail about God's role and our responsibility:

What God Has Done

His divine power has given us everything we need for life and godliness through our knowledge of him who called us by his own glory and goodness. Through these he has given us his very great and precious promises, so that through them you may participate in the divine nature and escape the corruption in the world caused by evil desires (verses 3,4).

What We Must Do

> For this very reason, make every effort to add to your faith goodness; and to goodness, knowledge; and to knowledge, self-control; and to self-control, perseverance; and to perseverance, godliness; and to godliness, brotherly kindness; and to brotherly kindness, love. For if you possess these qualities in increasing measure, they will keep you from being ineffective and unproductive in your knowledge of our Lord Jesus Christ. But if anyone does not have them, he is nearsighted and blind, and has forgotten that he has been cleansed from his past sins (verses 5-9).

God has given us everything we need for life and godliness. He has equally distributed Himself to all His children because every Christian has been made a partaker of His divine nature. Our responsibility is to make every effort to add on to our faith the character qualities of goodness, knowledge, self-control, perseverance, godliness, brotherly kindness, and love. If we do so, we will live effective and awesome lives. The people who don't do this have forgotten that they are alive in Christ and dead to sin. What should they do? Try harder? No! They should affirm again their faith foundation of who they are in Christ and commit themselves to their growth in character: "Brethren, be all the more diligent to make certain about His calling and choosing you; for as long as you practice these things, you will never stumble" (2 Peter 1:10 NASB).

All that we have received from God has eternal value. "We are God's workmanship" (Ephesians 2:10). And "his incomparably great power" (Ephesians 1:19) is at work in us to produce a new creation. The biblical teachings that various aspects of God's nature are given to the believer is strong evidence that sanctification is truly the work of God. God comes into the believer and transforms him by His very presence. Sanctification is the increasing experience of life or eternal life, of which God is the only source (see Psalm 36:9; John 17:3; Ephesians 4:18).

Another aspect of love is correction. God disciplines us so that we may share in His holiness. In the book of Hebrews we are told, "Endure hardship as discipline; God is treating you as sons. For what son is not disciplined by his father? . . . Our fathers disciplined us for a little while as they thought best; but God disciplines us for our good, that we may share in his holiness" (Hebrews 12:7,10). God does not punish us for doing something wrong; He disciplines us for our good in order to share in His holiness. Our holiness comes from sharing in His holiness. Man has no source of holiness in himself apart from Christ.

Becoming a partaker of God's holiness does not mean that we have become God or a god. Rather, we receive a holiness that is like God's—a holiness that will produce righteousness and peace. In the Bible we are told to "make every effort to live in peace with all men and to be holy; without holiness no one will see the Lord" (Hebrews 12:14).

While God the Father is the primary agent in our sanctification, Christ and the Holy Spirit also have roles. All three members of the trinity have a part in making us holy.

Christ's Role in Our Sanctification

Jesus came that we might have life. To make that possible, He had to first die for our sins. At the moment of salvation, believers are joined to Christ so that *He* is their life. The oft-repeated phrases "in Christ," "in Him," and "in the beloved" all mean that our soul is in union with God.

They indicate that we are right now alive in Christ. Every aspect of Christian ministry is dependent upon this awesome truth because apart from Christ we can do nothing. Paul wrote, "For this reason I have sent to you Timothy, who is my beloved and faithful child in the Lord, and he will remind you of *my ways which are in Christ,* just as I teach everywhere in every church" (1 Corinthians 4:17 NASB, emphasis added).

There are no verses in the Bible that instruct us to pursue power because we already have power in Christ. Paul said in Ephesians 1:18,19, "I pray also that the eyes of your heart may be enlightened in order that you may know the hope to which he has called you, the riches of his glorious inheritance in the saints, and his incomparably great power for us who believe."

Pursuing something you already have can only lead you down the wrong road. Power for the Christian is found in the truth, and the power of the devil is in the lie. If you expose Satan's lies, you will destroy his power because he truly is a defeated foe. Satan has deceived the whole world (Revelation 12:9); consequently, the world lies in the power of the evil one. However, Satan can't do anything about your position in Christ. But if he can get you to *think* that your position in Christ isn't for real, then you will live as though it isn't. "Our struggle is not against flesh and blood, but against the rulers, against the authorities, against the powers of this dark world and against the spiritual forces of evil in the heavenly realms" (Ephesians 6:12). It cannot be overstated how important it is to know who we are in Christ. The apostle John makes that point in 1 John 5:18-20 (NASB):

> We know that no one who is born of God sins;
> but He who was born of God keeps him and the
> evil one does not touch him. We know that we are

of God, and the whole world lies in the power of the evil one. And we know that the Son of God has come, and has given us understanding, in order that we might know Him who is true, and we are in Him who is true, in His Son Jesus Christ. This is the true God and eternal life. Little children, guard yourselves from idols.

The continuing process of sanctification is a walk with God in Christ. Notice what Jesus said in the greatest invitation ever extended to mankind: "Come to me, all you who are weary and burdened, and I will give you rest. Take my yoke upon you and learn from me, for I am gentle and humble in heart, and you will find rest for your souls. For my yoke is easy and my burden is light" (Matthew 11:28-30). Jesus didn't say come to the synagogue or submit to some program. He said, "Come to me"—come to My presence and I will give you rest. There is a "Sabbath-rest for the people of God; for anyone who enters God's rest also rests from his own work" (Hebrews 4:9,10). This much-needed rest is practicing the presence of God and living by faith in the power of the Holy Spirit. If we try to serve the Lord by walking according to the flesh, we will burn out.

When Jesus taught spiritual principles, He often used illustrations that the people of His day could relate to. He often used illustrations related to carpentry because He was raised in the home of a carpenter. Carpenters in those days fashioned yokes and doors, both of which the Lord used to speak of Himself. The yoke in Matthew 11:28-30 refers to a heavy wooden beam that fit over the shoulders of two oxen. The only way the yoke could work was if both oxen were in it and pulling together. If only one tried to use the yoke, it would be a chafing and binding affair. When a farmer had to break in a new ox, he would place it in a yoke with an older, seasoned ox who had learned obedience from the things he experienced (see Hebrews 5:8). The older ox knew it had a whole day of work ahead and knew better than to run when he should be walking. He knew better than to stray off to the left or to the right, since such sidetracks only led to more work later on down the path.

A young ox often becomes restless because he thinks the pace is a little slow, so he may try to run ahead, only to burn out before noon. And if he is tempted to stray off to the left or to the right, he will get a sore neck from the yoke. It doesn't take long for a young ox to realize that maybe the older ox knows what he is doing, so it's best to settle down and learn from the one who knows where he is going and how to get there.

What do we learn from all this? To take one day at a time. To learn the priority of relationships. And to learn the graceful ways of God.

> Do you not know? Have you not heard? The LORD is the everlasting God, the Creator of the ends of the earth. He will not grow tired or weary, and his understanding no one can fathom. He gives strength to the weary and increases the power of the weak. Even youths grow tired and weary, and young men stumble and fall; but those who hope in the LORD will renew their strength. They will soar on wings like eagles; they will run and not grow weary, they will walk and not be faint (Isaiah 40:28-31).

The Holy Spirit's Role in Our Sanctification

References in the Bible that teach that progressive sanctification is done by the Holy Spirit are few. Some of these referring to the Spirit's sanctifying work seem to emphasize only the positional aspect—that is, the person is set apart unto God by the work of the Spirit. For example, Paul says in 2 Thessalonians 2:13, "From the beginning God chose you to be saved through the sanctifying work of the Spirit and through belief in the truth."

Yet, it's clear that Paul *does* directly attribute the continuing process of sanctification to the Holy Spirit (1 Thessalonians 4:3-8). In verse 3 it is stated that God has called us to be sanctified. In verses 7 and 8 we read that God has called each of us to not be impure but to live a holy life. Verse 8 goes on to connect the presence of the Holy Spirit to Paul's discussion about our sanctification: "Therefore, he who rejects this instruction does not reject man but God, who gives you his Holy Spirit."

Jesus, in His recognition and concern that we still live in a fallen world, prayed this to the Father: "My prayer is not that you take them out of the world but that you protect them from the evil one. They are not of the world, even as I am not of it. Sanctify them by the truth; your word is truth" (John 17:15-17). It is the Holy Spirit who leads us into all truth (John 16:13). This may be the greatest ministry of the Holy Spirit, who is first and foremost "the Spirit of truth" (John 14:17). As we will see in the next chapter, truth is the means by which we are sanctified.

The work of our sanctification, then, has all of its source in God. It involves the Father, the Son, and the Spirit in their usual working relationship as the trinity. We could say that 1) the Father is the initiator of sanctification; 2) Christ is the mediator whose saving work in death and resurrection provides the basis for our sanctification; and 3) it is the Holy Spirit who actually comes into all creation to sustain and enliven it. He is the one who indwells the believer to apply the sanctifying work of Christ and bring personal union with all the members of the trinity.

Our Role in Our Sanctification

Since we are what we are by the grace of God, and He is the primary agent of our sanctification, should we simply let go and let God take care of making us holy? Is allowing God to do His job the only role we play in our sanctification? The Bible clearly teaches that's not the way it is. Both man and God have a part. In the Old Testament passage Leviticus 20:7,8 we read: "Consecrate [sanctify] yourselves and be holy, because I am the LORD your God. Keep my decrees and follow them. I am the LORD, who makes you holy [sanctifies you]." The same truth is taught in the New Testament in Philippians 2:12,13: "Continue to work out *your* salvation with fear and trembling, for it is *God* who works in you to will and to act according to his good purpose" (emphasis added). While it's true that we are saved when we are born again and placed in Christ, still we are told to be actively involved in our restoration to wholeness or holiness.

Later in Philippians, Paul describes his own activity in his growth in terms of a runner: "Brothers, I do not consider myself yet to have taken hold of it. But one thing I do: Forgetting what is behind and straining toward what is ahead, I press on toward the goal to win the prize for which God has called me heavenward in Christ Jesus" (Philippians 3:13,14). This prize is the completion of our sanctification, our conformity to Christ.

Doing Our Part

There's a story about a pastor who found great joy in gardening. On a rare day off, one of his deacons found him working in his garden.

"My, the Lord sure gave you a beautiful garden," he said to the pastor.

"Well, thank you very much," the pastor responded, "but you should have seen it when God had it to Himself!"

In a similar way, when it comes to sowing and harvesting for God's kingdom, the Lord has chosen to allow us to participate in His work.

The church, which is comprised of all believers, has something in common with an electrical appliance store. Every appliance is created for a specific purpose, but not one can accomplish anything without electricity. They come in all shapes and colors, but they will never fulfill their purpose unless they receive power from a generating station. By themselves they don't even make good furniture or household decoration. But with the flip of a switch they are all energized in order to fulfill their purpose. The toaster makes toast, the coffeemaker brews coffee, and the refrigerator preserves our food and keeps our Dr Pepper cold. It would be foolish to say one appliance is better than the other, for they were all designed with a different purpose in mind.

That's true for Christians as well. Jesus said, "You are the light of the world. A city on a hill cannot be hidden. Neither do people light a lamp and put it under a bowl. Instead they put it on its stand, and it gives light to everyone in the house. In the same way, let your light shine before men, that they may see your good deeds and praise your Father in heaven" (Matthew 5:14-16). The

Lord will receive no glory if we don't do good deeds or let our light shine. Neither will He receive any glory if we draw attention to ourselves by trying to find a meaningful existence without being plugged in to Him.

A Combined Effort

How much will be accomplished for the glory of God in this present church age if we try to do everything by ourselves? Nothing! How much will be accomplished if we sit back in "holy piety" and expect God to do it all? Apparently nothing because God has committed Himself to work through the church:

> His intent was that now, *through the church,* the manifold wisdom of God should be made known to the rulers and authorities in the heavenly realms, according to his eternal purpose which he accomplished in Christ Jesus our Lord. In him and through faith in him we may approach God with freedom and confidence (Ephesians 3:10-13, emphasis added).

We are told to "put on the Lord Jesus Christ, and make no provision for the flesh in regard to its lusts" (Romans 13:14 NASB). What if we don't actively take our place in Christ? What if we make provision for the flesh? We are told to put on the armor of God, but what if we don't? We are told not to use our bodies as instruments of wickedness (Romans 6:12,13), but what if we do? We are told to take every thought captive to the obedience of Christ (2 Corinthians 10:5)—but what if we don't? At best we will surely stop bearing fruit; at worst we will be utterly defeated and separated from God.

Because God Works, We Work

We are saved by faith and sanctified by faith, but faith without works is dead. According to James:

> What good is it, my brothers, if a man claims to have faith but has no deeds? Can such faith save him? . . . Faith by itself, if it is not accompanied by action, is dead. But someone will say, "You have faith; I have deeds." Show me your faith without deeds, and I will show you my faith by what I do (James 2:14,17,18).

A story is told about a young man who approached the foreman of a logging crew and asked for a job.

> "Do you have a job I can do?" asked the young man.
>
> "That depends," replied the foreman. "Let's see you fell this tree."
>
> The young man stepped forward and skillfully felled a great tree. Impressed, the foreman exclaimed, "You can start Monday."
>
> Monday, Tuesday, Wednesday, and Thursday rolled by—and Thursday afternoon the foreman approached the young man and said, "You can pick up your paycheck on the way out today."
>
> Startled, the young man replied, "I thought you paid on Friday."
>
> "Normally we do," said the foreman. "But we're letting you go today because you've fallen behind. Our daily felling charts show that you've dropped from first place on Monday to last place today."
>
> "But I'm a hard worker," the young man objected. "I arrive first, leave last, and even work through the coffee breaks!"

> The foreman, sensing the young man's integrity, thought for a moment and then asked, "Have you been sharpening your ax?"
>
> The young man replied, "No sir. I've been working too hard to take time for that!"[2]

Our lives are like that. We need to do good works, and to do good works we need to sharpen up on the truth of God's word. If a person is truly a Christian, then it will be demonstrated by how he or she believes and lives. What a person does is a reflection of what he or she has chosen to believe.

In the Bible, the works of sanctification are termed as "our" or "your" righteousness and works—that is, the works are those of the believer and not just God. For example, Deuteronomy 6:25 says, "It shall be *our* righteousness, if we observe to do all these commandments" (KJV, emphasis added). Paul says that the one who supplies you with the seeds to sow will "enlarge the harvest of *your* righteousness" (2 Corinthians 9:10, emphasis added). He also talks about "*your* work produced by faith" (1 Thessalonians 1:3, emphasis added). John says, "He who does what is right is righteous" (1 John 3:7).

In the process of sanctification, we are yoked together with Christ, and we must pull together under His direction and by His power. According to Ephesians 2:10, our good works are already prepared, but we must walk in them. The fact that God's work is prior and primary means that sanctification is ultimately a matter of faith, just as justification is. We are not departing from the sphere of faith when we move from justification to sanctification. We are not justified by faith and then sanctified by works. If we took that route, Paul would probably rise out of his grave and say again, "You foolish [people]! Who has bewitched you? . . . I would like to learn just one thing from you: Did you receive the Spirit by observing the law, or by believing what you heard? Are you so foolish? After beginning with the Spirit, are you now trying to attain your goal by human effort?" (Galatians 3:1-3).

What Christ Does and What We Do

The biblical teaching about sanctification includes the wonderful truth that Christ's work in salvation is substitutionary. His sinless life and His death were *for* us as a substitute. But *the Spirit's* work in *applying* the fruit of Christ's substitution is not done as a substitute. Rather, God works *in* us to will and to do, but He does not will and do *for* us (see Philippians 2:13). We must actively exercise our will and do good works.

The truth of what Paul says in Galatians 2:20 ("I no longer live, but Christ lives in me...") cannot be interpreted as substitutionary in the sense that Christ lives my life *instead* of me. Somehow Christ lives in me and yet I also actively live. Paul continues, "...The life I live in the body, I live by faith in the Son of God, who loved me and gave himself for me" (Galatians 2:20). The "I" that continues to live is still intact but is now complete in Christ. Sanctification, then, is actually the restoration of true selfhood. As such, it calls the human faculties of personhood (mind, emotion, and will) into action so that they may be exercised and grow in holiness. God does not trample on our humanness; He sets us free in Christ to be fully human.

What we are saying is that our thinking, our feeling, and our active willing are part of us. These capacities must be renewed in sanctification. And God cannot renew them without working through them, which means they must be active. Thus, we must believe and obey by thinking, feeling, and choosing. These cannot be carried along passively because part of us wouldn't be functioning and, thus, would be left out of our total renewal. For example, there is no other way to renew a will than through the exercise of that will. It's at that point that God somehow renews a person by challenging him and providing the power for him to actively use his will and other capacities.

The Heart's Place in Sanctification

The prophet Ezekiel challenged his listeners to "get a new heart and a new spirit" (Ezekiel 18:31), yet he knew that people are dependent on God for this to happen. God Himself said in Ezekiel 11:19, "I will give them an undivided heart and put a new spirit in them; I will remove from them their heart of stone and give them a heart of flesh." Later, in Ezekiel 36:26, He said, "I will give you a new heart and put a new spirit in you." From these passages we can clearly see that the new heart and spirit are gifts from God, and yet we are called to have a part in receiving these gifts.

Jeremiah brings together our relationship with God and the gift of a new heart in Jeremiah 24:7: "I will give them a heart to know me, that I am the LORD. They will be my people, and I will be their God, for they will return to me with all their heart." This is a heart to know and experience God. In the new covenant, which every child of God is privileged to be under, the Lord says,

> I will put My law within them, and on their heart I will write it; and I will be their God, and they shall be My people. And they shall not teach again, each man his neighbor and each man his brother, saying, "Know the LORD," for they shall all know Me, from the least of them to the greatest of them (Jeremiah 31:33,34 NASB).

The heart is the real person and the place from which all life comes (Proverbs 27:19; 4:23). The heart is thus the place of personhood, intellect, emotion, and will. And God's covenant promise is a changed heart: "I will make an ever-lasting covenant with them: I will never stop doing good to them, and I will inspire them to fear me [literally, put the fear of me in their hearts], so that they will never turn away from me" (Jeremiah 32:40). We also see this reflected in Paul's prayerful words, "May the Lord direct your hearts into God's love and Christ's perseverance" (2 Thessalonians 3:5).

Sanctification is the process of changing the heart, which is actually a change of the total person (that is, the mind, emotion, and will or actions). The Bible portrays the heart as the center where all these elements of personhood come together. Not only do these elements come together in the heart, they also cannot be separated within the heart. We will explore how truth must penetrate the heart in order to touch our emotions and behaviors, but first we must understand that sanctification is *total*—the *whole* person is involved.

The Heart and Our Intellect

Contrary to popular thinking, the main function of the heart is not emotional. The heart, according to the Bible, is: first—the place where the human being thinks; second—where he wills; and third—where he feels. Check out what H. Wheeler Robinson found. He counted 822 uses of the word *heart* for some aspect of human personality. According to his categorization, 204 of the 822 uses refer to intellectual activity, 195 to the making-a-choice aspect, and 166 to an emotional state.[3]

A good illustration of this kind of usage for the word heart is seen when Moses says to the Israelites, "To this day the LORD has not given you a heart to know, nor eyes to see, nor ears to hear" (Deuteronomy 29:4 NASB). Just as the eyes are for seeing and the ears are for hearing, so also is the heart for knowing. When Job wants to tell his "friends" that he is not inferior to them in understanding, he literally says, "I have a heart as well as you." The New American Standard version translates this, "I have intelligence as well as you" (Job 12:3). The "man of heart" in the Bible is not a man of deep feeling, but a man "of understanding" (Job 34:10,34).

The mind is the thinking function of the heart.

While most think of the heart as the seat of emotion, the verses we just looked at show it's more accurate to understand the heart as the seat of reflection. The essential business of the heart is stated in Proverbs 15:14: "The mind [literally, heart] of the intelligent seeks knowledge" (NASB).

Many mental functions are related to the heart. We believe with the heart (Romans 10:10; Hebrews 3:12); we meditate with the heart (Psalm 19:14; 49:3); we consider and worry in the heart (Psalm 14:1; 15:2; Luke 12:29; Romans 10:6); and that which we memorize is kept in the heart (Psalm 119:11; Proverbs 6:21; Luke 2:51).

The Old Testament consistently uses the word *heart* for the place of thinking because the Hebrew vocabulary had no other word for mind. The New Testament connects the concept of the mind with the heart in several places. This suggests that the mind is, in reality, the thinking function of the heart. Despite the use of a different word for "mind" in the New Testament, the mind still represents the intellectual function of the heart.

The Heart and Our Will

In addition to being the place where we think, the heart is also the place where we will or purpose. We desire and choose in our hearts. David rejoiced in God because he said God had given him the desire of his heart (Psalm 21:1,2). When God tested his people in the wilderness, Moses told the people it was "to know what was in your heart, whether or not you would keep his commands" (Deuteronomy 8:2). God looked at their hearts to see whether they would choose to obey or not. That's because the heart is the place of all purposes and plans, all motives and intentions, and all resolutions.

Other than the presence of God in our lives, the capacity to choose is the greatest power that we possess. We can choose to believe or not believe. We can choose to walk by the Spirit or walk by the flesh. That's why we can say that successful Christian living lies in the exercise of the will.

The Heart and Our Emotions

The heart is also the place where we experience emotion. Love and hate, joy and sorrow, courage and fear, and all other emotions are viewed as being in the heart. For example, we are to love God with all our heart (Deuteronomy 6:5); shout joyfully to Him with a glad heart (Isaiah 65:14); and keep our heart from being troubled by believing in Christ (John 14:1).

Emotions are not simply experiences of the inner person. They are felt physically, especially in the heart. The Old Testament vividly expresses emotions as movements of the heart. If a person loses courage, his heart quivers like leaves in the wind (Isaiah 7:2); it is faint (Deuteronomy 20:8 NASB); it melts like wax (Psalm 22:14); it turns to water (Joshua 7:5). Fear is described in terms of a person's heart sinking (Genesis 42:28); failing (Psalm 40:12); being lost (1 Samuel 17:32). By contrast, courage is the strengthening of the heart (Psalm 27:14).

The relationship between the emotions and the physical body is the reason Scripture teaches that even physical health is affected by our emotional states. For example, in Proverbs 14:30 we read, "A heart at peace gives life to the body, but envy rots the bones." Nehemiah affirmed that positive emotions are truly healing to the body when he said, "The joy of the LORD is your strength" (Nehemiah 8:10).

The heart, then, is the place of knowing, willing, and feeling. It is the center of our personality. It is the place where God addresses us and from which we respond as whole persons. That is why its function of knowing stands first—for the ultimate function of the heart is to seek wisdom and knowledge by paying attention to God's Word.

It's All in the Heart

We often conceive of thinking, feeling, and willing as separate functions. For instance we may characterize someone as a "brain," "left-brained," or "cerebral," suggesting that he or she is heavy on reason and light on emotion—like Spock in the Star Trek movies. Or perhaps we say someone has a tendency to live primarily from his or her emotions without thinking. But these kinds of separations are contrary to biblical thought. Thinking, feeling, and willing all come together in the heart.

In the Bible, to "know" something is to grasp it in such a way that it affects the total personality. For the soul or heart to be stirred and led, the person is not only thinking, but he or she has also accessed the emotions and the will. An interesting example of knowledge involving the will or actual behavior is seen in Isaiah's statement, "An ox knows its owner, and a donkey its master's manger, but Israel does not know, My people do not understand" (Isaiah 1:3 NASB). Even though donkeys and oxen are not very intelligent, they know who cares for them and respond accordingly. But Israel did not know its Master.

Acknowledging that thought, emotion, and will are united within the heart is critically important for understanding Bible passages that talk about our knowledge of God and His knowledge of us (Matthew 7:22,23; John 10:27; Galatians 4:9). That is why eternal life can be described as knowing God through His Son Jesus Christ (John 17:3). It is this understanding of "know" that also makes sense of our Lord's promise that "you will know the truth, and the truth will set you free" (John 8:32). So often believers know the truth, but they are not free. That's because they do not know the truth in their *hearts*—they do not know it emotionally and behaviorally, as well as intellectually. It is a truth, but it's not their truth.

Sanctification in Summary

God is the primary agent of our sanctification because He gave us a new heart so that we would turn toward Him. When we do, we become an agent in our own sanctification, and our heart is conformed to the image of God. It is in the heart that our mind, emotions, and will are united in Christ-centered living. When we turn our hearts toward God, we begin to love Him and others.

Sold Out

2 Peter 1:3-9, John 10:10; Matthew 11:28-30

Reflect

According to 2 Peter 1:3-9, what has God done to provide for our sanctification? What is our responsibility in the sanctification process?

"God doesn't punish us for doing something wrong; He disciplines us." Explain the difference.

Jesus plays a role in our sanctification. At the moment of salvation, believers are joined to Christ so that He is their life. Why is this union essential to our sanctification?

What can Satan accomplish in the lives of believers if they don't know their position—who they are in Christ? How confident are you about your position in Christ? If you're unsure, review the "Who Am I?" list on pages 123–26 and memorize the verses that speak to your heart.

Respond

Almighty God and heavenly Father, I'm thankful that I'm not in this process of sanctification alone. I'm thankful that You called me Your child and that You called me to live a holy life. I see in Your Word how every part of You is at work in me: Father, Son, and Holy Spirit. You make possible the miracle of sanctification. I know I have a role to play as well, and I ask You to help me live above sin and not carry out the desires of the flesh but to live a life of faith and dependence on You. I want to stay yoked to You, Jesus, and to follow You. I want to keep in step with the Spirit. I unite my heart—mind, will, and emotions—to You Jesus, to serve You and others. I pray this in Your name, Jesus. Amen.

Do not conform any longer to the pattern of this world, but be transformed by the renewing of your mind. Then you will be able to test and approve what God's will is—his good, pleasing and perfect will.

—ROMANS 12:2

Transformed!

I like the story of the little boy who fell out of bed. When his mom asked him what happened, he answered, "I don't know. I guess I stayed too close to where I got in." It's easy to do the same with our faith. It's tempting just to stay where we got in and never move.[1]

— *Max Lucado*

A high school student at a Christian retreat at the YMCA camp in Estes Park, Colorado, wrote me a letter after hearing several messages about her identity in Christ and how to win the battle for the mind. Like so many students, she indicated in her letter the trouble we have renewing our minds and winning the battles. We tend to look to some spiritual feeling or experience to ensure our freedom rather then the truths that Jesus proclaims about us. Here is part of what she shared:

Dear Mr. Park,

I just wanted to let you know how much I appreciated your speaking. I know that the talks you gave really touched the lives of a lot of people—I know that because they really touch me.

I enjoyed the weekend, not because I had any kind of euphoric spiritual or emotional "high" (I've had plenty of those—they fade 2 days after you get home), but because I was able to realize in my heart what I'd known for too long only in my head. I'd heard the verse James 4:7 so many times, but I didn't really understand what "resist the devil" meant, nor did I understand what it meant to "take every thought captive."

My mind is a battleground, territory won over by Christ, and the negative, lying thoughts are like enemy spies trying to take over. I can't just passively listen to them anymore because they'll destroy me from within.

What freedom to know in my heart what used to be only head knowledge: that Jesus has changed me and is changing me and using me in spite of my selfish desires. I know this is a continuing process, but also that through Him I'm not a sinner but a saint (who still sins).

I wasn't brought to tears last weekend, but I'm now more alert and battle-ready than I ever have been. And that's really exciting!

This past weekend I also witnessed God's working in the lives of my friends in incredible ways. It was such a privilege for me to be able to see that!

Again, thanks for your messages last weekend!

Your sister in Christ!

Reprogramming Our Minds

The truth will indeed set us free and transform our character. To understand how, we need to start by realizing that a greater change took place when we were born again spiritually than will take place when we die physically. Salvation isn't addition; it is transformation. As Christians, we are both physically and spiritually alive as long as we reside on planet Earth. When we die physically, we will be absent from the body and present with the Lord. Our old physical bodies will return to dust, and we will receive resurrected bodies, for flesh and blood cannot inherit the kingdom of God (1 Corinthians 15:50-54). Until then, Paul tells us not to use our bodies as instruments of unrighteousness because if we do we allow sin to reign there. We are urged by the mercies of God to present our bodies to Him as living sacrifices (Romans 12:1). Paul then encourages us to be transformed by the renewing of our minds (12:2). Before we came to Christ, our minds were programmed to live without God. In progressive sanctification, we have the responsibility to reprogram our minds to the truth of God's Word.

Like a computer, our brains record the experiences we have in life. Newborn babies come into this world with a clean slate. The only world they know is what they can see, hear, feel, taste, and smell. Nothing has been programmed into their computer. They have no vocabulary and, therefore, no way to communicate with those who are charged to take care of them. They have neither the presence of God in their lives nor the knowledge of His ways. So during their early and formative years, they learn to live independently of God. In later years, when these little gals and guys come to Christ, their minds are still programmed to live without God. There is no delete or clear button that can be pushed to get rid of old thinking patterns. That's why they need to renew (reprogram) their minds.[2]

It takes time to renew our minds and replace the lies we have believed with the truth of God's Word. Yet that should not bum us out or discourage us, for we have all the resources we need to make that happen. The Lord has given us the Holy Spirit, who is the Spirit of truth (John 14:17), and He will guide us into all truth (John 16:13). Also, because we are one with God, "we have the mind of Christ" (1 Corinthians 2:16). And finally, Paul tells us we have superior weaponry available to us for winning the battle for our minds:

> Though we live in the world, we do not wage war as the world does. The weapons we fight with are not the weapons of the world. On the contrary, they have divine power to demolish strongholds. We demolish arguments and every pretension that sets itself up against the knowledge of God, and we take captive every thought to make it obedient to Christ (2 Corinthians 10:3-5).

Read the same passage from The Message:

> The world is unprincipled. It's dog-eat-dog out there! The world doesn't fight fair. But we don't live or fight our battles that way—never have and never will. The tools of our trade aren't for marketing or manipulation, but they are for demolishing that entire massively corrupt culture. We use our powerful God-tools for smashing warped philosophies, tearing down barriers erected against the truth of God, fitting every loose thought and emotion and impulse into the structure of life shaped by Christ. Our tools are ready at hand for clearing the ground of every obstruction and building lives of obedience into maturity (2 Corinthians 10:3-5).

Paul is not talking about defensive armor; he's talking about battering-ram weaponry that tears down strongholds that have been raised up against the knowledge of God. A stronghold is a negative pattern of thinking that has been burned into our minds either by repeating the action over and over or because of certain traumas we have experienced.

The Problem of Strongholds

How are these strongholds erected in our minds? This programming of our minds is said to take place in two ways. The first is through experiences that we had in early childhood—such as the family we were raised in, the churches we went to, the neighborhoods where we grew up, the communities we belonged to, the friends we had, and so on. These external factors all had an effect upon how we perceive reality, and they shape our attitudes about ourselves and others.

It isn't just the environment, however, that determines how we develop. Two children can be raised in the same home, have the same parents, eat the same food, have the same friends, go to the same church, and respond differently. For instance, Jacob and Esau were born of the same mom, but they were very different in their temperaments and personalities. Our environment isn't all that shapes us because every one of us has a different way of interpreting the world we live in. In addition, God has created each of us unique, in a way that He planned even before the foundation of the world (Ephesians 1:4; 2:10).

Along with the prevailing experiences we have had, the second greatest contributor to the development of strongholds are traumatic experiences. For instance, you may have been abused when you were a child; you may have had parents who didn't get along and are divorced; or perhaps someone close to you died unexpectedly. These kinds of experiences are not deeply rooted into our minds over time; but are burned into our minds quickly because of their intensity.

All of our experiences have been stored in our memory like a file in our computer. Consequently, all kinds of mental strongholds have been raised up that block out the knowledge of God. And at the moment of salvation, there is no "clear" button to delete all the information strongholds that have been programmed into our minds.

As we struggle to reprogram, or renew, our minds, we are also confronted daily with a world system that is not godly. Remember, Paul warned us to "not conform any longer to the pattern of this world" (Romans 12:2). Obviously we can continue, even as Christians, to allow the world we live in to affect our minds. That is why Paul also warned, "See to it that no one takes you captive through hollow and deceptive philosophy, which depends on human tradition and the basic principles of this world rather than on Christ" (Colossians 2:8).

Even though we have the Spirit of truth to lead us, we can still choose to follow the ways of the world. The right and the responsibility to choose is the greatest power we possess other than the presence of God in our lives. We can choose to pray or not pray, to read our Bibles or read books that aren't edifying. Every child of God can choose to walk by the Spirit or walk by the flesh. We choose who we will serve.

> England has a constitutional queen and a prime minister. The queen has no power to make political, governmental decisions; she is simply a figurehead. The prime minister, on the other hand, is

the one who leads the political process that makes the governmental decisions and holds the power.

Jesus Christ can be just the constitutional King of your life, or He can be the Prime Minister of your life, having the power to lead you where He would have you go. The choice is yours![3]

Dealing with Temptation

Because we live in this world, we are always going to face the reality of temptation. Keep in mind, however, that *it is not a sin to be tempted.* If that were so, then the worst sinner who ever lived would be Christ because He "has been tempted in every way, just as we are" (Hebrews 4:15). Yet Jesus was without sin.

When Satan wants to tempt you, he knows exactly which buttons to push. He knows your weaknesses. The things that may tempt you may not tempt other people at all. And Satan's goal with temptation is to get all of us to live our lives independently of God—that is, to walk according to the flesh rather than the Spirit (see Galatians 5:16-26). We need to be on guard, ready to battle temptation at all times:

> A young Native American boy felt he was ready to become a man. The chief of the tribe said, "To become a man, you must first survive in the high mountains for one week. If you survive, then you will be considered a man."
>
> So the little boy set out for the mountains on his quest to become a man. Climbing to the highest mountain, he noticed a rattlesnake lying in a patch of snow.
>
> The young boy was startled when the snake spoke to him. "Please help me," said the shivering snake. "I am cold, lost and far from home. Please pick me up and carry

me back to the valley where it is warm. If I stay here, I will surely die."

The boy drew close, but was careful not to get too close because he knew that this kind of snake was very deadly.

"I know your kind," said the boy. "You will only bite me when I pick you up."

The snake said, "Oh, but I won't bite you. I will be your friend if you will carry me down the mountain. You can trust me."

The boy thought it over and decided that any snake that could talk must be a special kind of snake. So he picked up the snake and carried him all the way down to the warm valley. He gently placed the snake on the ground, and immediately the snake coiled up and struck the boy on the neck.

The boy cried out with a scream, "You bit me! You promised that you wouldn't bite me. Now I'm going to die!"

With an evil hiss, the snake slithered off into the grass and said, "I can't help that. You knew exactly what I was when you picked me up. So long, sucker."

That's the way sin is. It tempts us and draws us close. It tells us lies. It persuades us to go against our better judgment and to handle it. It convinces us to not believe that it will surely kill us. That is when sin is most deadly—when we think it's our friend.[4]

Some people think a good way to deal with temptation is to shut themselves off from the world. But that's not a realistic option, nor is that Christ's calling for us. Besides, even if we did try to shut out the world, we would still face temptation because there is so much junk already programmed into our memory banks that we could be tempted for years without having to leave our homes. This is especially true in the area of sexual temptation. Once sexual strongholds are formed in the mind, the mental impressions are there for instant recall.

The Bible warns us about temptation, but also gives us hope:

> So, if you think you are standing firm, be careful that you don't fall! No temptation has seized you except what is common to man. And God is faithful; he will not let you be tempted beyond what you can bear. But when you are tempted, he will also provide a way out so that you can stand up under it (1 Corinthians 10:12,13).

If we are going to take the way of escape that God provides for us, we must take our thoughts captive to the obedience of Christ. If we allow tempting thoughts to rumble around in our minds, we will eventually take a path that leads to destruction. The apostle James tells us this about temptation:

> When tempted, no one should say, "God is tempting me." For God cannot be tempted by evil, nor does he tempt anyone; but each one is tempted when, by his own evil desire, he is dragged away and enticed. Then, after desire has conceived, it gives birth to sin; and sin, when it is full-grown, gives birth to death (James 1:13-15).

Understanding the New Man

The Mind and the New Man

To better understand how temptation affects us, please refer to the following diagram featuring the new man. The

Bible says we have an outer man and an inner man (2 Corinthians 4:16). The outer man is the physical body, which relates to the world. The physical brain is a part of the outer man. The mind, on the other hand, is a part of the inner man. There is a big difference between the brain and the mind: The brain is organic matter. When we die physically, the brain will return to dust. We will be absent from the body and present with the Lord, but we will not be mindless.

The brain functions much like a digital computer that has millions of switching transistors that code all the information in a binary numbering system of 0's and 1's. In a similar fashion, every neuron in the brain operates like a little switch that turns on and off. Each neuron has many inputs (dendrites) and only one output that channels the neurotransmitters to other dendrites.

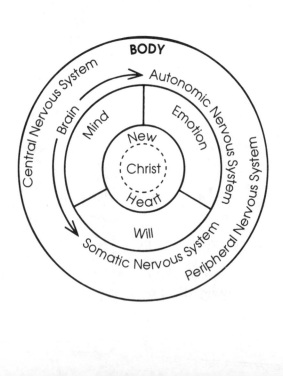

Millions upon millions of these make up our computer hardware, the brain. Our minds, on the other hand, represent the software. The brain receives data from the external world through the five senses of the body. The mind is the compiler and chooses to interpret the data by whatever means it has been programmed to use. Until we come to Christ, our minds are programmed by external sources and internal choices made without the knowledge of God or the benefit of His presence.

The tendency of the Western world is to assume that mental problems are primarily caused by faulty hardware (the brain). There is no question that Alzheimer's disease and problems such as chemical or hormonal imbalances can interfere with our abilities to function. The best software program won't work if the computer is turned off or in disrepair. However, our primary problem is not the hardware, it is the software. Other than submitting our bodies to God as living sacrifices and taking care of ourselves physically, we can do little to fix the hardware, but we *can* change the software. Now that we are alive in Christ, we have been given the mind of Christ, a new heart, and the Holy Spirit to lead us into all truth.

The Nervous System and the New Man

The brain and the spinal cord make up the central nervous system, which splits off into a peripheral nervous system (as shown in the previous diagram). The peripheral nervous system has two channels: the autonomic and the somatic nervous systems. The somatic nervous system regulates our muscular and skeletal movements, such as speech and gestures. In other words, that which we have willful control over.

How Our Thoughts Affect Us

Our autonomic nervous system regulates our glands, which we have no willful control over. We don't say to our heart, "Beat, beat, beat," or to our adrenal glands, "Adren, adren, adren," or to our thyroid, "Thy, thy, thy." They function automatically. In a general sense, we don't have control over our emotions either. You cannot will yourself to like someone you find emotionally unattractive. We do, however, have control over what we think (and do), and we *can decide* to believe that what God says is true. Just as our glands are regulated by our central nervous system, so also are our emotions a product of our thoughts. It is not the circumstances of life that determine how we feel. Rather, how we feel is basically determined by how we interpret the events of life. Between the event and our emotional response is our brain (the receiver) and our mind (the interpreter). That is, our brains and minds check out the world around us, and our emotions respond to that information. (In chapter 9 we'll look at this interaction between the mind, will, and emotions in more detail.)

Let's apply all this to the problem of stress. When life pressures put demands on our physical system, our adrenal glands respond by secreting cortisonelike hormones into our physical body. This causes the natural "fight or flight" response to the pressures of life. If the pressures persist too long and our adrenal glands can't keep up, then our stress becomes distress. The result can be physical illness or irritability about things that wouldn't bother us physically or emotionally in less stressful times.

This raises a key question: Why is it that two people can respond differently to the same stressful situation? Some teens actually thrive under pressure, while others fall apart. Do some people have superior adrenal glands? We don't think so. Although every person may differ considerably in his or her physical makeup, the major difference isn't in the biological factors. We all face the pressures of tests, deadlines, schedules, traumas, and temptations. The major difference is in the software—that is, how we mentally interpret the world and process the information our brains are receiving.

When we encounter a difficulty, our minds can choose to respond by trusting God and His assurance of victory or by viewing ourselves as the helpless victims of circumstances. For instance, the Israelite soldiers saw Goliath in reference to themselves and became stressed out. Young David saw the same giant in reference to God and triumphed in the situation that had left experienced soldiers in defeat.

Faith in God greatly affects how we interpret and respond to the pressures of this world. And no matter what happens in life, we can *always* rest in the assurance that "in all things God works for the good of those who love him, who have been called according to his purpose" (Romans 8:28).

The Power of Choice

Our sex glands are also part of the autonomic nervous system. They function apart from the will and regulate normal sexual functioning according to our sexual identities. Our God-given sexual functionings and identities are not the cause of sexual immorality or the lack of self-control. But if we load up our minds with pornographic images and use our bodies as instruments of unrighteousness, we will drive our sex glands into overload. We *do have control* over what we choose to think, believe, and do.

When we allow our minds to be stimulated externally or by recalling experiences that we have had, an autonomic signal causes a hormone called *epinephrine* to be secreted into the bloodstream, which locks into our memory whatever stimulus is present at the time of the emotional excitement. This reaction causes us to involuntarily remember emotionally charged events—negative and traumatic as well as positive ones. That is why pornographic images and experiences can remain in our memories for months and even years, whereas boring academic facts that we've had to study can fade from our minds before the final exam is given. The positive benefit of this is that thinking of good memories can result in a more positive mood. (To understand more about freedom from sexual addiction, see Neil and Dave's book *Purity Under Pressure*.)

In every tempting situation we have a choice. We can respond according to the flesh (the way we learned to respond before we came to Christ) or we can respond according to the Spirit. Galatians 5:17 tells us the two are in opposition to each other because the flesh is programmed to live independently of God and the Holy Spirit is dependent upon God the Father. How do you know which one you have chosen? "The deeds of the flesh are evident" (Galatians 5:19 NASB; see also verses 20 and 21), and so is the fruit of the Spirit (Galatians 5:22,23). Our countenance and behavior reveal the choices we make.

Suppose you choose to walk according to world principles and standards. If you continue to do that for about six weeks, you will establish a habit that leads to the formation of a stronghold that hinders your commitment to God and your desire to follow His principles.

There are a countless number of strongholds that have been raised against the knowledge of God. The philosophies of this world have affected the way we think, which affects the way we feel, which results in less-than-godly character. Sanctification works the opposite way. It begins by our receiving forgiveness, the life of Christ, and a new heart. It continues as we renew our minds by choosing the truth, which affects our emotions and transforms our character.

Positional sanctification assures us that we are a new creation in Christ, and we need to daily appropriate that truth by faith. Progressive sanctification is based upon the foundation that we are already children of God and that the "inner man is being renewed day by day" (2 Corinthians 4:16 NASB). At the same time, we are still contending with the world, the flesh, and the devil. Because we were created in God's image, we have the capacity to choose whom we will serve—the god of this world or the one and only Creator of all things. Much of progressive sanctification is the struggle to overcome external influences and the internal mental strongholds raised up against the knowledge of God. We overcome them by the internal presence of God and the external help of the body of Christ. Wholeness and true mental health comes when we choose the truth, appropriate it by faith, and walk by the Spirit.

Sold Out

Read

Romans 12:1,2; 2 Corinthians 10:1-5; James 1:13-16;
Galatians 5:16-23

Reflect

According to Romans 12, what action do we need to
take? What does God do? Who do you think is transforming us?

What are strongholds? How are they created in our
minds?

Many of the experiences that are stored in our minds
have been built into strongholds. What can we do to
break these strongholds down?

It's not a sin to be tempted. But when does temptation become sin? How can we overcome temptation?

Why do we need to take the truth and apply it daily?
What happens when we don't?

What is the choice we have as believers?

Respond

Dear Lord, You said in Your Word not to be like this
world, think like this world, or do the things that this
world does. I confess that I have followed the world
and have given into its evil ways. I choose now to
present myself to You and be transformed by the
renewing of my mind. I choose to stay close to You
and Your Word. I want to do Your will, Lord, and
experience your peace, the peace You say is beyond
understanding. In Jesus' name I pray, amen.

Then you will know the truth, and the truth will set you free .

—JOHN 8:32

My prayer is not that you take them out of the world but that you protect them from the evil one.... Sanctify them by the truth; your word is truth.

—JOHN 17:15,17

Truth in Jesus has a living influence on our hearts.[1]

—*John Eadie*

Truth: That's What Sets You Apart!

In our ministry, Neil and I (Dave) have met with many young people who are struggling with their thoughts and have heard voices in their minds. One of our ministry's surveys revealed that seven out of ten Christian young people are hearing voices in their minds—like each of them has a subconscious self talking to him or her. Is the problem physical or spiritual? Every case is different, but one thing is certain: No manipulation of drugs in kind or quantity can cure a mentally sick person if the problem is in the software and not the hardware.

This brings up a very important question: What is mental health? Mental health experts define mental health as being in touch with reality and relatively free of anxiety. Those are reasonable standards, but anyone caught in a spiritual battle for his or her mind would fail on both counts. We believe that mentally healthy people are those who have a true knowledge of God, know who they are as children of God, and have a balanced biblical worldview that includes the reality of the spiritual world. If you knew that God loved you, you were forgiven, He had gone before you to prepare a place for you for all eternity, you didn't need to fear death, and you had the peace of God guarding your heart and mind, would you be a mentally healthy person? Of course you would! But mentally ill people usually have a distorted concept of God and a terrible perception of themselves. (If you don't believe that is true, then visit a psychiatric ward. You'll find some of the most religious people you have ever met, but their concept of God and themselves is very distorted.) We believe that taking medicine to cure the body is commendable, but taking drugs to cure the soul is deplorable.

The reality presented in Scripture is defined more fully than the reality of the world. Actually, the Bible presents the unseen spiritual and eternal world as more real than the temporary world we now see and exist in: "We fix our eyes not on what is seen, but on what is unseen. For what is seen is temporary, but what is unseen is eternal" (2 Corinthians 4:18).

God *is* the truth and the *revealer* of truth. The total concept of truth includes both what is real and what is trustworthy. Anything that is opposed to God and His revelation is a lie. True life, according to Scripture, can come only through living in harmony with God and His will.

The "natural man" (the person who has not accepted Christ) is spiritually dead; he is separated from God. His mind has been programmed by the world, and, consequently, his heart is deceitful. Paul says, "The man without the Spirit does not accept the things that come from the Spirit of God, for they are foolishness to him, and he cannot understand them, because they are spiritually discerned" (1 Corinthians 2:14). On the other hand, "We know that we are children of God, and that the whole world is under the control of the evil one. We know also that the Son of God has come and given us understanding, so that we may know him who is true. And we are in him who is true—even in his Son Jesus Christ. He is the true God and eternal life" (1 John 5:19,20).

The Trinity and Truth

In a previous chapter we saw that every member of the Godhead is the source of our sanctification and life. Every one of these primary agents is also described as *true* or *truth*. (In the verses that follow, we have italicized these keywords for emphasis.)

The prophet Jeremiah tells us, "The LORD is the *true* God; he is the living God" (10:10). Jesus prays, "This is eternal life: that they may know you, the only *true* God" (John 17:3). (Notice the connection Jesus makes between truth and life.) The psalmist says God is the "God of *truth*" (Psalm 31:5). John says, "God is *truthful*" (John 3:33).

God is true, and what He says is true—whether or not fallen humanity believes Him. Paul raises the question, "What if some did not have faith? Will their lack of faith nullify God's faithfulness?" Then he answers it, "Not at all! Let God be *true*, and every man a liar." (See Romans 3:3,4.)

Christ, the ultimate revelation of God, is the truth incarnate. "The Word became flesh and made his dwelling among us. We have seen his glory, the glory of the One and Only, who came from the Father, full of grace and *truth*" (John 1:14). Jesus said, "I am the way and the *truth* and the life" (John 14:6). He is the way to God because He is the truth, and the truth is life. Paul says, "Surely you heard of him and were taught in him in accordance with the *truth* that is in Jesus" (Ephesians 4:21). When Jesus completed His work, He said, "I will ask the Father, and he will give you another Counselor to be with you forever—the Spirit of *truth*" (John 14:16,17). Later, He added, "When he, the Spirit of *truth*, comes, he will guide you into all *truth*" (John 16:13). The Holy Spirit is God dwelling in believers to actually carry on the work of sanctification and holiness in their lives.

The Truth Is What Changes Us

Over and over the Bible teaches that we are changed or sanctified by the truth. It is the truth that brings people to God and then bears fruit in them: "The word of *truth*, the gospel that has come to you . . . this gospel is bearing fruit and growing, just as it has been doing among you since the day you heard it and understood God's grace in all its *truth*" (Colossians 1:5,6, emphasis added). "From the beginning God chose you to be saved through the sanctifying work of the Spirit and through belief in the *truth*" (2 Thessalonians 2:13, emphasis added). Paul also tells of those who refuse "to love the *truth* and so be saved" (2 Thessalonians 2:10, emphasis added).

As believers we are to "live by the *truth*" (1 John 1:6; the NASB says "practice the *truth*"). Paul says, "You were taught, with regard to your former way of life, to put off your old self, which is being corrupted by its deceitful desires; to be made new in the attitude of your minds; and to put on the new self, created to be like God in *true* righteousness and holiness" (Ephesians 4:22-24, emphasis added). The latter part of verse 24 is more literally "in righteousness and holiness of the *truth*" (NASB).

As Christians, then, we have the truth and the life within us. This means we can recapture lost ground as we are being renewed in the inner man. Let's look at the basic elements in the diagram we saw on page 172 and see how progressive sanctification gradually renews the mind and heals damaged emotions as the will is led by the Spirit.

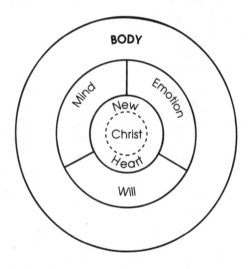

Overcoming the effects of the world, the flesh, and the devil is possible only because of our co-crucifixion with Christ. First, we are *crucified to the law*: "Through the law I died to the law so that I might live for God. I have been crucified with Christ and I no longer live, but Christ lives in me. The life I live in the body, I live by faith in the Son of God, who loved me and gave himself for me" (Galatians 2:19,20).

Second, because of the great work of Christ, we have been *crucified to the world*. Paul said, "May I never boast except in the cross of our Lord Jesus Christ, through which the world has been crucified to me, and I to the world" (Galatians 6:14). We still live *in* this fallen world, but we are no longer *of* it. Our citizenship is in heaven.

Third, we have been *crucified to sin*: "We know that our old self was crucified with him so that the body of sin might be done away with, that we should no longer be slaves to sin—because anyone who has died has been freed from sin" (Romans 6:6,7). All this has been accomplished for us by Christ.

Fourth, by our own conscious choice, we have *crucified the flesh*: "Those who belong to Christ Jesus have crucified the flesh with its passions and desires. Since we live by the Spirit, let us keep in step with the Spirit" (Galatians 5:24,25). Romans 8:13,14 tells us, "If you live according to the flesh, you will die; but if by the Spirit you put to death the misdeeds of the body, you will live, because those who are led by the Spirit of God are sons of God." Death is the ending of a relationship, not the ending of an existence. The world, the devil, and the flesh still exist, but we have a new relationship in Christ, who has overcome all the adversaries that would keep us in bondage.

Putting Off the Old Man

Renewing our mind begins with genuine repentance. John the Baptist preached, "Repent and believe the good news!" (Mark 1:15). Luke says of Jesus, "Then he opened their minds so they could understand the Scriptures. He told them, 'This is what is written: The Christ will suffer and rise from the dead on the third day, and repentance and forgiveness of sins will be preached in his name to all nations, beginning at Jerusalem'" (Luke 24:45-47).

Repentance literally means a change of mind, but in the Bible it means more than just changing your mind. It is a *change of attitude,* which implies a change that affects the whole person. When some Pharisees and Sadducees went to John the Baptist to be baptized, John said, "You brood of vipers! Who warned you to flee from the coming wrath? Produce fruit in keeping with repentance." (Matthew 3:7,8). John discerned that their repentance was not genuine. They wanted the blessings of God without giving up their habits, traditions, customs, worldly positions, and religious practices.

When giving a profession of faith, the early church converts would stand, face the west, and make the following public declaration: "I renounce you, Satan, and all your works and all your ways." Every work of Satan had to be renounced for repentance to be complete. These converts understood the necessity of renouncing all the evil practices and beliefs that had been going on in their synagogues, families, and personal lives. The early church preached, "Repent, then, and turn to God, so that your sins may be wiped out, that times of refreshing may come from the Lord" (Acts 3:19). Paul said to Agrippa, "I preached that they should repent and turn to God and prove their repentance by their deeds" (Acts 26:20). Peter said the Lord doesn't want "anyone to perish, but everyone to come to repentance" (2 Peter 3:9).

Repentance is the first step in renewing our minds. Without repentance, the effects of the old self are still dominant. Progressive sanctification is then stalled because we are still believing the lies of this world even though we're professing to believe the truth. People who are expressing faith in God but manifest no substantial change in their lives are caught between two kingdoms. They are *in* the kingdom of light, but they still believe the father of lies. Satan cannot do anything about our position in Christ, but if he can get us to believe that it isn't for real, we will live as though it isn't.

In one of the old Andy Griffith TV shows, Otis, the town drunk, got a letter telling him that he was to receive a large amount of money. There was one catch. He had to go for an interview and prove that he was worthy to receive the money.

Andy and Barney helped Otis get ready for his interview. They sobered him up, shaved him, got him a haircut, and bought him a new suit. He looked like a completely new person. He went for the interview and was given the money. But a few days later he came stumbling back into the jail, as drunk as a skunk. He hadn't shaved; his new suit was a mess. What happened? Nothing! That's right—nothing! Nothing happened *inside* Otis. He was still the same drunk he was before. He had only been temporarily cleaned up on the outside.[2]

Unless Otis changes on the inside first (repents) he will always return to his old behavior. Otis is a fictional character, but so many young people are just like him: They don't know who they are in Christ and aren't willing to truly repent by changing their minds and attitudes about sin.

The Lie Kills

Satan blatantly opposed the truth of God when he said, "You will not surely die" (Genesis 3:4). Adam and Eve believed the lie. The result? Mankind dies. This first sin reveals the true picture of all sin. It stems from the lie and leads to the destruction of true life. The effects are seen in guilt, fear, shame, alienation, misery, and death (3:7-24).

Jesus is the truth and the author of life. Satan is the father of lies and author of death. Satan's lies are the *roots* of all sins; thus, it is the root of murder. The devil "was a murderer from the beginning, not holding to the truth, for there is no truth in him" (John 8:44). It's also interesting to note that Jesus' enemies sought to kill Him because they would not receive the truth (verses 40,45). If we choose to believe Satan's lies, we will sin.

The connection between the lie and unrighteousness and the consequence (death) is also emphasized in the book of Romans: "The wrath of God is being revealed from heaven against all the godlessness and wickedness of men who suppress the truth [divine reality] by their wickedness" (Romans 1:18). This passage demonstrates that truth is a power that can have life-transforming effects. Even our "small" lies have direct consequences.

> A lawyer came to town. He was in a new town, with a new office, but no clients. When he saw someone coming to his office, he immediately picked up the phone and said, "I'm flying to New York on the MacKensie case. It looks like a biggie. And bring Grace in from New Jersey on the Indigo case. Also, I may be joining Anderson, Park, and Saucy as a partner. Gotta go now, someone just walked in." With that he hung up the phone, turned to the man, and said, "Now may I help you?"
>
> The man replied: "I'm here to hook up the phone!"[3]

Many people, like the lawyer, ignore the truth or hold it back, and the result is that they are affected by the opposite of truth—the lie. *Lies always catch up with you.* The lie results in godlessness and wickedness, which brings the wrath of God and, finally, death.

Sin's Deceitfulness

The real disease of the heart is its deceitfulness (Jeremiah 17:9). The basic connection between sin and the lie is also seen in the relationship between sin and deceit. Notice how Paul brings this out in the following verses: "Sin... deceived me" (Romans 7:11); "every sort of evil...deceives those who are perishing" (2 Thessalonians 2:10); "encourage one another . . . so that none of you may be hardened by sin's deceitfulness" (Hebrews 3:13). The outcome of sin's connection with the lie and deceitfulness is that mankind is killed and destroyed. Sin cheats us of life, which is found in the truth of Jesus Christ. The real battle is between Christ and the Antichrist, good and evil, the truth and the lie, divine revelation and satanic deception, the father of lies and the one true God.

The Battle for the Mind

This battle is going on for the hearts and minds of every person, young or old, created in the image of God—both believers and unbelievers. Satan blinds the minds of unbelievers (2 Corinthians 4:4), and Paul says to believers, "I am afraid, lest as the serpent deceived Eve by his craftiness, your minds should be led astray from the simplicity and purity of devotion to Christ" (2 Corinthians 11:3 NASB). Paul also says, "The Spirit clearly says that in later times some will abandon the faith and follow deceiving spirits and things taught by demons" (1 Timothy 4:1). Is that happening today? It is—all over the world.

As we've mentioned before, Neil and Dave have counseled hundreds of young people, in many cultures, who were struggling with their thoughts and having difficulty concentrating and reading their Bibles. In the more extreme cases, people were actually hearing voices. With few exceptions, these people were in a spiritual battle for their minds—a battle that can be resolved with complete repentance. (This process is outlined in Neil and Dave's book *The Bondage Breaker Youth Edition.*)

Remember our discussion regarding the power behind some mental/emotional stability? What is being passed off as mental illness oftentimes is nothing more than a battle for the mind. "You have a chemical imbalance," is the common medical explanation given to those who are hearing voices, being plagued with negative thoughts, having panic attacks, or struggling with chronic depression. The assumption is that the problem is physical (that is, a hardware problem), and a prescription is usually given in an attempt to correct the problem. While it's true that our body chemistry *can* get out of balance and hormonal problems *can* cause sickness and disorientation, we still have to ask questions that explore other possibilities. Possibilities such as: How can a chemical in the brain produce a personal thought? How can our neurotransmitters involuntarily and randomly fire in such a way as to create a thought that we are opposed to thinking? Is there a natural, medical explanation for that? Can the natural sciences be so sure about their answers when they haven't taken into account all reality—including the spiritual realm?

When troubled young people hear voices, what are they actually hearing? The only way we can hear a sound with our ears is if there is a physical source of that sound. A sound wave is a rhythmic compression of air molecules. Sound moves physically through the air and is picked up by our eardrums, which in turn sends signals to our brains. But the voices or disturbing thoughts that many people hear do not come from any kind of physical source. These people are often deemed mentally ill because, from a natural science perspective, they appear to be out of touch with reality, with the physical world around them.

What about young people who say they are seeing "things"? What are they actually seeing? The only way we can see something with our physical eyes is when light reflects off a material object. The spiritual world, however, doesn't have material substance, so we cannot see a spiritual being with our natural eyes or hear it with our ears. Remember, Paul says that "our struggle is not against flesh and blood, but against the rulers, against the authorities, against the powers of this dark world and against spiritual forces of evil in the heavenly realms" (Ephesians 6:12).

Girding Ourselves with the Truth

Our first line of defense against spiritual attacks upon our minds is to look to the truth. The armor of God, like any other armor, stops penetration, yet it cannot be appropriated passively. We have to actively take our place in Christ: "Put on the full armor of God, so that when the day of evil comes, you may be able to stand your ground, and after you have done everything, to stand. Stand firm..." (Ephesians 6:13,14).

When Jesus met with His disciples for the last supper, He prayed to the Father:

> My prayer is not that you take them out of the world but that you protect them from the evil one. They are not of the world, even as I am not of it. Sanctify them by the *truth*; your word is *truth*. As you sent me into the world, I have sent them into

the world. For them I sanctify myself, that they too may be truly sanctified (John 17:15-19, emphasis added).

We can't overcome the father of lies by human reasoning or by scientific research. We can only overcome the father of lies by God's revelation—His truth. That's why Paul tells us, "From the beginning God chose you to be saved through the sanctifying work of the Spirit and through belief in the *truth*" (2 Thessalonians 2:13, emphasis added).

The Word Is the Source of Truth

The Word Brings Life

Peter tells us, "Like newborn babies, crave pure spiritual milk, so that by it you may grow up in your salvation, now that you have tasted that the Lord is good" (1 Peter 2:2). The Word of God is for us what milk is to babies. Without milk, babies don't grow, and without the Word of God, neither do we. In addition, "The word of God is living and active. Sharper than any double-edged sword, it penetrates even to dividing soul and spirit, joints and marrow; it judges the thoughts and attitudes of the heart" (Hebrews 4:12).

God's Word has living power because the written Word of God cannot be separated from His person. As John tells us, Jesus is the Word incarnate (John 1:1,14). God's Word is the expression of His mind, and the expression of His mind is the expression of His person. Thus His Word is the expression of His omnipotent self. Earlier we learned that it was by His word (or the expression of His mind) that creation came into being:

"By the word of the LORD were the heavens made" (Psalm 33:6).

In the Old Testament, God assured His chosen people of success if they meditated on His Word (Joshua 1:8). And in Psalm 119, we find many references to the life-changing quality of the Word:

> "How can a young man keep his way pure? By living according to your word" (verse 9).

> "I have hidden your word in my heart that I might not sin against you" (verse 11).

> "I delight in your decrees; I will not neglect your word" (verse 16).

> "Preserve my life according to your word" (verses 25,37).

> "I will walk about in freedom, for I have sought out your precepts" (verse 45).

> "Direct my footsteps according to your word" (verse 133).

Psalm 19:7 says, "The law of the LORD is perfect, reviving the soul." The concept of "reviving" in the Hebrew language means "cause me to live." Psalm 107:19,20 says, "They cried to the LORD in their trouble, and he saved them from their distress. He sent forth his word and healed them; he rescued them from the grave." The Lord said through the prophet Isaiah, "My word . . . goes out from my mouth: It will not return to me empty, but will accomplish what I desire and achieve the purpose for which I sent it" (Isaiah 55:11). There is life, power, and direction in the Word of God. Jesus said, "The Spirit gives life; the flesh counts for nothing. The words I have spoken to you are spirit and they are life" (John 6:63).

The Word Has Power

If it's truth that sanctifies us, and God's Word is truth, then there is tremendous power in the Word. This can be illustrated on a much smaller scale by the power of human words. Scripture declares that "death and life are in the power of the tongue" (Proverbs 18:21 NASB) and "a soothing tongue is a tree of life, but perversion in it crushes the spirit" (Proverbs 15:4 NASB). James also reveals the destructive power of words: "The tongue also is a fire, a world of evil among the parts of the body. It corrupts the whole person, sets the whole course of his life on fire, and is itself set on fire by hell" (James 3:6). That's why Paul warns us, "Do not let any unwholesome talk come out of your mouths, but only what is helpful for building others up according to their needs, that it may benefit those who listen" (Ephesians 4:29). The next two verses say that we grieve the Holy Spirit when we use our words to tear down rather then build up. If every person could put into practice Ephesians 4:29, I'm sure that many of our problems would disappear overnight.

Finding God's Truth

Sanctification takes place when we appropriate the truth. But where is the truth found? First, God's truth can be revealed to us through nature. This can be seen in rainbows (Genesis 9:12-17) and in creation itself (Psalm 19:1-4; Romans 1:20). In Romans 1:19-21, Paul states that *all* people know something of the truth of God: "What may be known about God is plain to them, because God has made it plain to them....God's invisible qualities...have been clearly seen, being understood from what has been made, so that men are without excuse. For although they knew God, they neither glorified him as God nor gave thanks to him." The sinfulness within the hearts of unsaved people causes them to try to suppress God's truth (verse 18)—but that truth cannot be suppressed.

God's truth is also revealed in our moral nature (Romans 2:14,15). He has written His truth in the hearts of all people—even the hearts of unbelievers. Thus, all people have some knowledge of God's truth. Though an unbeliever's heart will try to resist this truth, it cannot be totally silenced. God's moral truth speaks constantly (even to unbelievers) because it is what compels us to create some semblance of moral order through government and laws.

For the believer, truth is revealed through the Spirit's presence as a witness within the heart (Jeremiah 31:33). Our conscience, which is a function of the mind, is not yet perfect and, thus, not a source of perfect truth. The conviction of the Holy Spirit, however, *is* infallible and works in the believer's heart to move him or her to God's truth.

Truth is also revealed through other believers' lives. Every Christian displays God's truth in his or her life (2 Corinthians 3:1-3; 1 Thessalonians 1:6,7). This is especially true of mature Christians (1 Corinthians 11:1; Hebrews 13:7; 1 Peter 5:3). Their example of a changed life is an important witness of truth.

The most important place we can find truth, of course, is in God's Word—in His special revelation, which provides standards for us by describing God and His works—and is, thus, the place of canonical truth (Psalm 119:43,142,151,160; John 17:17; 2 Timothy 2:15; James 1:18).

The Central Truths of Sanctification

Within the Bible are central truths that are essential to a believer's understanding and growth. These include: 1) the truths related to our salvation, including what God has already done for us and what He will do; and 2) the commands that reveal how we as Christians should live. These commands for living are based on what is already true about our salvation and the absolute assurance of what is yet to come because of our salvation. The beginning point of sanctification is belief in the gospel—believing what God has done for us in salvation. This entails what He has done in the past and what He will do for us in the future. By faith we rest in the finished work of Christ. *Faith is a choice to trust in Christ,* to believe that He did for us what we couldn't do for ourselves. Faith is the operating principle of life.

Our sanctification is dependent upon believing the truth of who we are in Christ, resting in His finished work, and then living out the truth of our new position in Christ. According to Romans 6:11, we are to choose to believe that we are alive in Christ and dead to sin.

Growing in Truths That Apply Today

We believe that God's desire for us in the ongoing process of sanctification is for us to experience who we really are in Christ. This means choosing to believe who we are as children of God on a daily basis. To help you in this process, here is a list to remind you of your identity:

SINCE I AM IN CHRIST
BY THE GRACE OF GOD...

Romans 5:1: I have been justified, completely forgiven.

Romans 6:1-6: I died with Christ and died to the power of sin's rule over my life.

Romans 8:1: I am free from condemnation.

1 Corinthians 1:30: I have been placed into Christ by God's doing.

1 Corinthians 2:12: I have received the Spirit of God into my life that I might know the things freely given to me by God.

1 Corinthians 2:16: I have been given the mind of Christ.

1 Corinthians 6:19,20: I have been bought with a price. I am not my own; I belong to God.

2 Corinthians 1:21,22: I have been established, anointed, and sealed by God in Christ.

2 Corinthians 5:14,15: I have died. I no longer live for myself, but I live for Him.

2 Corinthians 5:21: I have been made righteous.

Galatians 2:20: I have been crucified with Christ. It is no longer I who live, but Christ lives in me. The life I am now living is Christ's life.

Ephesians 1:3: I have been blessed with every spiritual blessing.

Ephesians 1:4: I have been chosen in Christ before the foundation of the world to be

holy and without blame before
Him.

Ephesians 1:5: I was predestined (determined by
God) to be adopted as God's son
or daughter.

Ephesians 1:7, 8: I have been redeemed, forgiven, and
am a recipient of His lavish grace.

Ephesians 1:13,14: I have been given the Holy Spirit as
a pledge (a deposit/down pay-
ment) guaranteeing my inheritance to come.

Ephesians 2:4,5: I have been made alive together with
Christ.

Ephesians 2:6: I have been raised up and seated
with Christ in heaven.

Ephesians 2:18: I have direct access to God through
the Spirit.

Ephesians 3:12: I may approach God with freedom
and confidence.

Colossians 1:13: I have been delivered (rescued) from
the domain of darkness (Satan's
rule) and transferred to the
kingdom of Christ.

Colossians 1:14; I have been redeemed and
2:13,14: forgiven of all my sins (the debt
against me has been canceled.

Colossians 1:27: Christ Himself is in me.

Colossians 2:6,7: I have been firmly rooted in Christ
and am now being built up in
Him.

Colossians 2:10:	I have been made complete in Christ.
Colossians 2:11:	I have been spiritually circumcised (my old, unregenerate nature has been removed)
Colossians 2:12,13:	I have been buried, raised, and made alive with Christ.
Colossians 3:1-4:	I have been raised up with Christ. I died with Christ; my life is now hidden with Christ in God. Christ is now *my* life.
2 Timothy 1:7:	I have been given a spirit of power, love, and self-discipline.
2 Timothy 1:9:	I have been saved and called (set apart) according to God's purpose.
Titus 3:5:	I have been reborn and renewed by the Holy Spirit.
Hebrews 2:11:	I am sanctified and am one with the Sanctifier (Christ). He is not ashamed to call me His brother or sister.
Hebrews 4:16:	I have a right to come boldly before the throne of God (the throne of grace) to find mercy and grace in time of need.
2 Peter 1:4:	I have been given exceedingly great and precious promises by God, by which I am a partaker of God's divine nature.[4]

Growing in Truths for the Future

Believing in the realities of our future is a powerful means to change. As life grows out of the seed in which it started and the soil in which it is planted, so it is drawn to the sun beyond it. Our effort to be holy as God is holy is fueled by the "living hope" that one day we will be like our Lord (see 1 Peter 1:3; 1 John 3:2,3). We will live in a new creation that Peter describes as "the home of righteousness" (2 Peter 3:13).

Be Encouraged

Jonas Salk, a great scientist and the discoverer of the vaccine against polio, understood the concept of being encouraging. He once was asked, "How does this outstanding achievement, which has effectively brought an end to the word polio in our vocabulary, cause you to view your previous 200 failures?"

His response (paraphrased) was, "I've never had 200 failures in my life. My family didn't think in terms of failure. They taught in terms of experiences and what could be learned. I just made 201 discoveries. I couldn't have made it without learning from the previous 200 experiences."

Winston Churchill, too, was raised with encouragement. He was not intimidated by error. When he made one, he simply thought the problem through again. Someone once asked him, "Sir Winston, what in your school experience best prepared you to lead Britain out of her darkest hour?"

"It was the two years I spent at the same level in high school," he replied.

"Did you fail?"

"No," replied Sir Winston. "I had two opportunities to get it right."[5]

Do you let your past sins intimidate you? Be encouraged; be positive! Churchill and Salk didn't focus on their failures; rather, they focused on the positive opportunities that were ahead. Start thinking about and believing the truths of God's grace and how you are established in that grace. While you meditate on what God has done for you, who you are in Christ, and your future hope, you must also hear and believe the commands given to you in Scripture. It is important to understand what these commands really are in relation to God's gracious work in salvation and the truth that sanctifies us. Our prayer for you is that you will learn how to establish yourself in God's truth so that you can *live* and *walk* and *grow* like the saint that you are.

Sold Out

Read

Colossians 1:5,6; 2 Thessalonians 2:13

Reflect

Renewing our minds begins with real repentance. How would you define repentance? Is it possible to renew our minds without repentance?

God is looking for a change that affects the whole person. How have your actions changed since you came to Christ? What actions or attitudes do you think still need to be changed?

Sanctification takes place when we appropriate truth. But where is truth found? Read out loud the list of Scripture "since I am in Christ by the grace of God" (pp. 196–98). Select three verses that speak to you and choose one to memorize.

Respond

Almighty God, Your Word reveals that You are truth. What You say is true whether I choose to believe it or not—but *I choose to believe Your Word*. I also ask You to give me a new appreciation for the power of the truth as well as the destructiveness of the lie. Help me to appropriate the armor You provide so I can stand strong against the lie. Also, please sensitize me to the revelation of Your truth in creation, my moral nature, the conviction of the Spirit, the lives of other believers, and Your written Word. Help me live according to Your Word as You use it to sanctify me. Finally, help me choose on a daily basis to believe who I am as Your child. I pray this in Jesus' name, amen.

Notes

The Refiner's Fire

1. Oswald Chambers, *Prayer, A Holy Occupation* (Nashville: Discovery House Publishers, 1992), p. 29.
2. Wayne Rice, "Nobel's Legacy," *More Hot Illustrations for Youth Talks* (Grand Rapids, MI: Zondervan Publishing House, 1995), p. 129.
3. The lyrics from "Refiner's Fire," written by Brian Doerksen, © 1990, are used by permission of Mercy/Vineyard Publishing.

Chapter 1: Awesome, Holy Design

1. Charles Swindoll, *Growing Deep in the Christian Life* (Portland, OR: Multnomah Press, 1986), p. 200.
2. Jim Burns and Greg McKinnon, "A Different Perspective," *Illustrations, Stories and Quotes You Can Hang Your Message On* (Ventura, CA: Gospel Light Publishing Co., 1997), p. 45.
3. Ibid., "Bumble Bee," p. 43.
4. Wayne Rice, "The Emperor's Seeds," *More Hot Illustrations for Youth Talks* (Grand Rapids, MI: Zondervan Publishing House, 1995), pp. 58-60.
5. Ibid., "Great Babies," p. 79.
6. Burns and McKinnon, "Some Things Are Immovable," *Illustrations, Stories and Quotes*, p. 47.
7. Rice, "The Queen of England," *More Hot Illustrations*, pp. 167-68.

Chapter 2: Totally Saved and Set Apart

1. Max Lucado, *When God Whispers Your Name* (Dallas: Word Publishers, 1994), p. 129.
2. Adapted from Neil Anderson, *Living Free in Christ* (Ventura, CA: Regal Books, 1993), pp. 56-58.
3. Story from Alice Gray, comp., *More Stories for the Heart* (Sisters, OR: Multnomah Publishers, Inc., 1997), pp. 278-81.

Chapter 3: Totally Holy

1. J.I. Packer, *Rediscovering Holiness* (Ann Arbor, MI: Servant Publication, 1992), p. 26.
2. Wayne Rice, "The Boy and the Circus," *Hot Illustrations for Youth Talks* (Grand Rapids, MI: Zondervan Publishing House, 1994), pp. 56-57.
3. Josh McDowell and Bob Hostetler, "Don't Be a Quisling," *Josh McDowell's One Year Book of Youth Devotions* (Wheaton, IL: Tyndale House Publishers, Inc., 1997), p. 365.

Chapter 4: A Radically Changed Relationship

1. Horatius Bonar, *God's Way of Holiness* (New York: Robert Carter and Brothers, 1865), p. 23.

2. Wayne Rice, "All-Points Bulletin," *More Hot Illustrations for Youth Talks* (Grand Rapids, MI: Zondervan Publishing House, 1995), p. 30.

3. Jim Burns and Greg McKinnon, "How About a Nice Swim to Hawaii?" *Illustrations, Stories and Quotes You Can Hang Your Message On* (Ventura, CA: Gospel Light Publishing Co., 1997), pp. 53-54.

4. Rice, "Excuse Me or Forgive Me," *More Hot Illustrations*, pp. 64-65.

5. Ibid., "Alligators in Your Pond," pp. 31-32.

6. Burns and McKinnon, "Prisoner of Sinful Desires," *Illustrations, Stories and Quotes*, p. 131.

7. Christian Mauer, *Theological Dictionary of the New Testament*, vol. 8, ed. Gerhard Friedrich (Grand Rapids, MI: Eerdmans, 1972), s.v. "accountable."

8. The being "made righteous" in this verse may refer to the future final ratification of the righteous standing of the believer. But whether present or future, our justification is always ultimately based on the obedience or righteousness of Christ and not on our own works of obedience.

9. Adapted from Wayne Rice, "Bought to Be Freed," *Hot Illustrations for Youth Talks* (Grand Rapids, MI: Zondervan Publishing House, 1994), pp. 52-55.

Chapter 5: A New You with a New Heart

1. D.A. Carson, "Matthew," in the *Expositor's Bible Commentary*, vol. 8, ed. Frank E. Gaebelin (Grand Rapids, MI: Zondervan Publishing House, 1984), p. 177.

2. Jim Burns and Greg McKinnon, "A Pardon: A Louisiana Court Case," *Illustrations, Stories and Quotes You Can Hang Your Message On* (Ventura, CA: Gospel Light Publishing Co., 1997), p. 179.

3. Ibid., "The Sheep-Lion," p. 69.

4. According to Hans Wolff, "The most important word in the vocabulary of Old Testament anthropology is generally translated 'heart,'" *Anthropology of the Old Testament* (Philadelphia: Fortress, 1974), p. 40.

5. Alice Gray, comp., "Beauty Contest," *More Stories for the Heart* (Sisters, OR: Multnomah Publishers, Inc., 1997), p. 92.

6. Bernard Ramm, *Offense to Reason: The Theology of Sin* (San Francisco: Harper and Row, 1985), p. 41.

7. Adapted from J. Knox Chamblin, *Paul and the Self* (Grand Rapids, MI: Baker, 1993), pp. 173-74.

Chapter 6: Making the New You Real

1. Elisabeth Elliot, *Shadow of the Almighty* (New York: Harper and Brothers, 1956), p. 15.

2. Bob Hostetler and Josh McDowell, "Don't Go Hunting for Honor," *Josh McDowell's One Year Book of Youth Devotions* (Wheaton, IL: Tyndale House Publishers, Inc., 1997), p. 162.

3. Richard N. Longenecker, "Galatians," *World Biblical Commentary*, vol. 41 (Dallas: Word Books, 1990), p. 156.

4. F.F. Bruce, "The Epistle to the Galatians," *The New International Greek Testament Commentary* (Grand Rapids, MI: Eerdmans, 1982), p. 186.

5. Neil Anderson and Dave Park, *Stomping Out the Darkness* (Ventura, CA: Regal Books, 1993), p. 41-43.
6. Josh McDowell and Bob Hostetler, "The Image on the Card," *Josh McDowell's One Year Book*, p. 147.
7. Alice Gray, comp., "Don't Forget What Really Matters," *More Stories for the Heart* (Sisters, OR: Multnomah Publishers, Inc., 1997), p. 154.
8. Jim Burns and Greg McKinnon, "Changed Lives," *Illustrations, Stories and Quotes You Can Hang Your Message On* (Ventura, CA: Gospel Light Publishing Co., 1997), pp. 143-44.

Chapter 7: Who's Changing You?

1. Durback, ed., *Seed of Hope*, A Henri Nouwen Reader (New York: Bantam Books, 1990), p. 197.
2. Wayne Rice, "Sharpen Your Axe," *More Hot Illustrations for Youth Talks* (Grand Rapids, MI: Zondervan Publishing House, 1995), p. 155.
3. From H. Wheeler Robinson, *The Christian Doctrine of Man* (Edinburgh: T. & T. Clark, 1926), p. 22.

Chapter 8: Transformed!

1. Max Lucado, *When God Whispers Your Name* (Dallas: Word Publishers, 1994), p. 141.
2. This illustration of the computer is not intended to deny that we are all born with a bent away from God. We have a clean slate only as far as information from outside. But we are born with a program that structures the input during our development years into habits and patterns of living for the self.
3. Jim Burns and Greg McKinnon, "Changed Lives," *Illustrations, Stories and Quotes You Can Hang Your Message On* (Ventura, CA: Gospel Light Publishing Co., 1997), p. 91.
4. Adapted from Wayne Rice, "The Native American and the Rattlesnake," *More Hot Illustrations for Youth Talks* (Grand Rapids, MI: Zondervan Publishing House, 1995), p. 125.

Chapter 9: Truth: That's What Sets You Apart

1. John Eadie, *Commentary on the Epistle to the Ephesians* (Grand Rapids, MI: Zondervan, n.d), reprint of 1883 ed. (Edinburgh: T. & T. Clark), p. 346.
2. Jim Burns and Greg McKinnon, "The Same Old Otis" *Illustrations, Stories and Quotes You Can Hang Your Message On* (Ventura, CA: Gospel Light Publishing Co., 1997), p. 85.
3. Adapted from ibid., "Big Shot Lawyer," p. 29.
4. Adapted from Neil Anderson and Dave Park, *Stomping Out the Darkness* (Ventura, CA: Regal Books, 1993), pp. 52-54.
5. Alice Gray, comp., "Another Chance," *More Stories for the Heart* (Sisters, OR: Multnomah Publishers, Inc., 1997), p. 77.

Neil T. Anderson

is the president of Freedom in Christ Ministries
and a much sought-after speaker on Christ-
centered living. He is the author of the
bestselling books *The Bondage Breaker*
and *A Way of Escape.*

Robert L. Saucy,

Distinguished Professor of Systematic
Theology at Biola University in La Mirada,
California, is the author of
The Church in God's Program.

Dave Park,

cofounder and executive director of
Freedom in Christ Youth Ministries,
speaks internationally to youth leaders,
parents, and teens. He is coauthor with Neil
Anderson of many books including
The Bondage Breaker Youth Edition, Extreme Faith,
Purity Under Pressure, and *Ultimate Love.*

Other Books by
Neil Anderson and Dave Park

The Bondage Breaker Youth Edition
The Bondage Breaker Youth Edition Study Guide
Stomping Out the Darkness
Stomping Out the Darkness Study Guide
Busting Free Youth Curriculum

FREEDOM IN CHRIST 4 TEENS
Devotional Series

Awesome God
by Neil Anderson and Rich Miller

Extreme Faith
by Neil Anderson and Dave Park

Reality Check
by Neil Anderson and Rich Miller

Ultimate Love
by Neil Anderson and Rich Miller

OTHER YOUTH RESOURCES
FROM FREEDOM IN CHRIST

Know Him, No Fear
by Rich Miller and Neil Anderson

FREEDOM IN CHRIST
ADULT AND STUDENT CONFERENCES

Stomping Out the Darkness
for high school and junior high students

The Seduction of Our Teens
Parent seminar will help parents make a lasting
spiritual impact at home

Setting Your Youth Free
Equips adults to have a powerful freedom ministry in the church

Purity Under Pressure
Helps students overcome sexual pressures
and establish godly relationships

Total Abandon
This prayer conference will help you hear the voice of God
and follow His leading

FREEDOM IN CHRIST YOUTH MINISTRIES
A Resource Ministry to Youth and the Church
Leading Teens, Parents, and Youth Leaders
to the Message of Freedom in Christ

For more information about having a
Freedom in Christ Ministries event in your area,
call, write, or e-mail:

Freedom in Christ Youth Ministries
16071 W. Sherman St.
Goodyear, AZ 85338

Phone: 623-925-5555
Fax: 623-925-1234
E-mail: davepark@integrityonline5.com
Website: www.ficyouth.com